How to be a 20-Minute Trader

How to be a 20-Minute Trader

An Essential Guide for All Traders in Any Market

Jeremy Russell

WILEY

For general information on our other products and services or for technical support,
please contact our Customer Care Department within the United States at (800)
762-2974, outside the United States at (317) 572-3993 or fax (317) 572-4002.

Wiley also publishes its books in a variety of electronic formats. Some content that
appears in print may not be available in electronic formats. For more information
about Wiley products, visit our web site at www.wiley.com.

Library of Congress Cataloging-in-Publication Data is Available:

ISBN 9781394205226 (Cloth)
ISBN 9781394205233 (ePub)
ISBN 9781394205240 (ePDF)

Cover Design: Wiley
Cover Image: © ATU Images/Getty Images

SKY10063509_122823

Contents

Foreword
by Sydney Koh

S itting in the parking lot of my son's school pickup line, I casually scrolled through my social media account. With a simple flick of my thumb, photos of friends' exotic travel adventures, adorable puppy videos, and the occasional ad for a work from home opportunity quickly zipped by. Facebook definitely knew me too well.

Then, out of nowhere, a particular ad caught my eye.

The 20-Minute Trader.

I smirked and immediately scoffed.

20-Minute Trader. Yeah, right. That's not a thing.

Back to the scroll.

Having been suddenly widowed at 41, I've explored various ways of making money online. Traditional employment was not a viable option for me as I had to raise my three elementary school-aged sons, one having special needs, as a solo parent.

I explored all the common ways of making money from home: affiliate marketing, online trading, agencies, publishing, and more. I found success in publishing as I used my personal experience in a dangerously toxic marriage to write several books to help those experiencing the same. However, I realized that having multiple income streams to support my young family would be beneficial for our long-term stability. So, my search for supplemental income continued.

The following day, a different ad for the 20-Minute Trader popped up on my feed. This time, a smiling gentleman calmly and casually explained the unique strategy of this trading system. I paused to listen to what he had to say as he was so obviously unlike the flashy young traders I've seen in the past. Without hyper cars or a mansion in the background, the man in the video, Jeremy Russell, held my attention and intrigued me.

Jeremy simply spoke of a particular pattern he noticed when he started trading and how he subsequently invested much time and capital in testing the reliability of this pattern. What he found and back-tested resulted in a surprising discovery that this pattern was highly predictable given some simple movements on the charts.

"Predictable" and "reliable" were the antitheses of my personal trading experience. What I've found in my time in the markets was very much the opposite. Jeremy's system was so different from what I have used before, and with the free course he offered, I decided there wouldn't be any harm to at least find out more.

A few simple clicks later, I learned more about this pattern, and as I did, I became increasingly curious. This was unlike any other pattern I have learned about in the past, and it excited me! No ascending wedges, no cup or handle, no Fibonacci sequences. This was just so different.

I learned that within the first 20 minutes of market open, if A happened, look out for B, and then execute the trade.

That's it? That's the pattern? That's the system?

It was as if my junk food–fueled, carnivorous teenage son just told me that not only has he decided to eat healthier, but that he is now a vegetarian. Yes, I was *that* shocked. Something that I had grown accustomed to and didn't question anymore was just entirely upended.

It was simple. Almost *too* simple. Surely, there must be more to it.

One thing I knew from my time trading was that I often had to babysit my trades. I hated being tied to my desk all day as I monitored the unavoidable rollercoaster of my active trades.

I was now even more curious about Jeremy's 20-minute trading system and soon found myself on the phone with the original 20-Minute Trader himself. We discussed my previous trading experience, and when he found out that most of my time in the markets was in swing trades, Jeremy exclaimed, "Wow, you're brave!"

On the other end of the phone line, I humbly smiled, misinterpreting Jeremy's comment as a compliment. A split second later, something didn't sit right with me. "Wait, hang on . . . what do you mean 'brave'?"

"Oh, I just mean that since you're holding trades overnight, you are willing to leave yourself exposed to overnight news."

Jeremy definitely had a point. One of the most annoying things about swing trading was that holding trades overnight during unpredictable news events or untimely government announcements beyond my control could significantly impact the profitability of my trades, either in a highly positive or highly negative manner. The latter proving to be disastrous, not to mention painfully expensive experiences.

It didn't take me long to recognize that I needed to learn more about the 20-Minute Trading strategy. The more I learned about this method, the clearer it became that this may be a game-changer in my trading journey.

Living in California meant I could start and end my trading day before my sons even woke up for school. No more being glued to my computer during market hours. Using this system would easily give me the additional stream of income I was seeking. Not only that, as I understood more about this strategy, I realized it would be fully scalable when I was ready to use more capital.

There is so much to appreciate about this trading system, and I hope you will explore it and come to the same conclusion that I did. This system simply works, and whether you are seeking to make a little extra in your monthly cash flow or considering using the system to generate significantly more income, it is worthwhile to invest the time to learn what it takes to become a successful 20-Minute Trader.

Best wishes and happy trading!

Sydney Koh

Author of *Dealing with the Unavoidable Narcissist in Your Life* and *Can't You Smell the Smoke?*

Introduction

Let's talk about patterns.

Michael Larson was an ordinary man from Ohio who became famous for his incredible win on the game show *Press Your Luck* in 1984. The show, hosted by Peter Tomarken, featured contestants answering trivia questions to earn spins on a large electronic game board known as the Big Board.

The Big Board had various prizes and cash amounts, but it also had a few squares that were labeled "Whammy." If a contestant landed on a Whammy, they would lose all their accumulated winnings and receive a comical animation of a cartoon character called the Whammy. The goal of the game was to accumulate as much money as possible without hitting a Whammy.

Michael Larson, an unemployed ice cream truck driver, became intrigued by the show's patterns during his extensive study of recorded episodes. He noticed that the random patterns on the Big

Board were not entirely random. The show used five different patterns that would cycle through randomly during each episode. Larson recognized that he could potentially memorize these patterns and predict the movement of the lights on the board.

In the spring of 1984, Larson made the decision to try his luck and become a contestant on CBS's *Press Your Luck*. He applied to be on the show and, after being accepted, traveled to Los Angeles for the taping.

During the show, Larson's strategy was to press the button to stop the flashing lights on the board at precise moments when he knew they would land on cash or prizes rather than Whammies. He successfully avoided the Whammies and managed to amass an astonishing amount of money.

Larson's approach was risky because if he hit a Whammy, he would lose all his winnings. However, he had meticulously memorized the patterns and was confident in his ability to anticipate the board's movements. As the game progressed, Larson's winnings grew rapidly, reaching unprecedented amounts. He won a total of $110,237 in cash and prizes, which was the largest one-day total in the history of daytime television at the time. In 2023 terms, this is over $330,000.

Larson's winning streak stunned the show's producers and staff, who suspected him of cheating. They reviewed the footage extensively but found no evidence of wrongdoing. Larson had simply exploited a flaw in the game's design and outsmarted the system.

The show's producers initially refused to pay Larson his winnings, alleging that he had cheated. Larson threatened legal action, and after several months of negotiations, he received his full prize money. The incident prompted the show to revise its game board patterns to make them more difficult to memorize and predict.

Michael Larson's incredible win on *Press Your Luck* made him a brief celebrity. Larson passed away in 1999 at the age of 49, leaving behind a legacy as one of the most memorable and controversial game show contestants in history.

Aside from identifying a pattern, another thing stands out about Larson. I suspect that Larson was not looking for the pattern when he watched this game show initially, but that it leapt out at him. For everyone else these flashes were random, with no discernable pattern, but to Michael, there was a pattern, a sequence. The lights shown in a specific series over exact periods. Hundreds of thousands had watched and many had played on this game show, and yet it seems no one but Michael saw this, or if they did, they decided not to monetize it.

When he first thought he had identified this pattern, he could have been a realist and simply said to himself, "I'm sure I can't predict this pattern. Someone would have noticed this by now," and refused to admit to himself that he was capable of knowing when these flashes would land in the winning squares.

But he didn't. He tested himself, recording episodes of the show in a beta or VHS VCR, playing it back, and learning how these predictable motions transpired.

That's how I felt in November 2019, never having looked at a single stock chart, or bought a single stock, or learned a single thing about the stock market . . . and yet I saw this thing happening that seemed completely obvious to me, in which a stock dropped and rose rather predictably, every day around the same time. I never thought it would help catapult a series of successes so soon after.

And here I am, just a random new trader. Not an ex–Wall Street fancy pants that had been apprenticed by Warren Buffet, or some super nerd who worships algorithms. I trade predictable patterns every day. In fact, as I write this sentence, I just looked at my account and noted that I made around $99,000 in the last three weeks of trading. In the last year, hundreds of thousands of people the world over have learned about the 20-Minute Trader, and perhaps by the time this book is published it will be millions.

Here's the weirder thing: I cannot even call myself an amateur on the subject of trading. If a Cub Scout learns first aid and you compare him to a doctor, I'm less educated at trading strategies than that kid is at medicine. I have no academic qualifications to consider myself an authority, and if you are looking for that, get a refund on this book before it's too late, and find someone with a PhD in trading who was on the floor of the New York Stock Exchange for years, or the Chicago Mercantile Exchange for decades. Someone who knows the Greeks, and the indicators, and the Relative Strength Index plus dozens of other formula . . . who has five screens around their desk facing their face. The only thing I trade with is a small laptop and my smartphone.

I know a few dozen or so words and symbols simply and precisely. I know how to buy and sell and some simple math. But the one ace-in-the-hole I have, that's best of all, is a way to predict a tiny jump in a stock price. I also know every single detail on how to explain this method in full.

What amazing code-breaking, glitch-causing method did I use to find this pattern? Actually, I did use a special technique, called NSBG. Have you heard of it? It's a very powerful technique. It stands for Non-Subconsciously-Biased Glancing.

Experts, PhDs, and philosophers down the ages have . . . never talked about this at all actually. I just made it up. But that doesn't mean it's not true.

Basically, I was glancing. And I noted it. Repeatedly.

We have all seen the phenomenon where a person, independent of the scene comes in, who knows nothing, notices something the whole company, family, group or civilization failed to notice, which was headlight-brightness obvious to them.

There's the story of the explorer who found a drought-stricken tribe, that had been there centuries, avoiding a nearby cave because it was occupied by an "evil demon." This was a collective certainty because the cave croaked out scary sounds continuously. It was therefore group knowledge that this cave was deadly dangerous, occupied by a demonic spirit that must be avoided, appeased, and feared. It was discussed and prayed about and dances were formed to fend off destructive effects. Committees, elders, and experts spoke on the matter with great authority, while the whole tribe was endlessly dehydrated due to no good water source. Children were taught at a young age to fear and avoid the cave (this actually sounds like the stock market to me, by the way, since "wise" elders naysay all new methods they see, and sneer at any innovation from new people).

This explorer decided, "I'll go inside and check it out," and found out it was an underground water source growling in its depths, as water churned in a whirlpool and mini-waterfall, echoing up to the mouth of the cave in deep grunts. He informed the tribe and solved their drought. And yet this mystical creature was a dominant factor in the lives of these people for possibly hundreds of years.

Now the drought was solved and the evil demon was gone. The explorer had employed NSBG, Non-Subconsciously-Biased Glancing. In other words, he wasn't subconsciously biased into believing in the demon. He just glanced with no preconceived ideas.

This was how I glanced at stock market charts.

I was 42, broke, just lost my job of 22 years and had no place so I was staying with my older brother, Kris, at the time, living in a spare bedroom he had. One day, I brought my laptop out and placed it on the coffee table.

I said, "Hey Kris, do you see that?" while pointing at the chart.

Kris is the first person who showed me stock charts a month earlier since he was experienced. He also introduced me to trading options.

"See what?" he asked, as he looked at the stock charts I showed him.

"I can tell you when that stock is going to go up," I said.

"Oh yeah, let's see," Kris said.

"Now," I said, and the line jumped up.

"Holy crap, you did it," he said.

Now you're about the throw this book out the window because people are paid millions and billions to predict market stuff, with the most detailed and complex algorithms in the universe, with an army of quantitative analysts dissecting everything in every detail. You don't want to hear the mutterings of some lucky idiot who stepped on a lottery mine by accident and who now thinks he's an expert.

I agree with you. I'd rather hear from a tried-and-true expert on anything. But let me be a little bit fair to myself.

And maybe I should be a little less self-deprecating about my lack of knowledge.

Since I released my methods in 2021, hundreds of thousands of people have learned about 20-Minute Trader pattern spotting in just a span of months with virtually no promotion from me. The main things they say is that they find the explanations refreshingly easy, applicable, and conceptually digestible. Ultimately, our students note that the 20-Minute Trader system is easy to understand and employ, especially when compared with the overly technical and often intentionally confusing voices in the trading world. I and my team have back-tested the 20-Minute Trader system extensively. I hired real pros to build a time machine and simulate the market in the past with software that reproduced the market exactly how it was down to the second, seeing if these patterns existed years ago. They did. Meanwhile, over the span of these three years, I read piles of books and thousands of pages of data about the Stock Market, interviewing dozens of traders both successful and unsuccessful.

I beta tested this pattern system with over 130 individual traders that I worked with personally. I recorded their results, obstacles, and successes and analyzed, polished, optimized, and published findings.

So, I might want to give myself a little break maybe and stop running myself down fully for being "uninformed." I am just traditionally uninformed. I did not study existing strategies, but I did study information, analytics, results, trends, symbols, words, and definitions. So, while I am an amateur or less when it comes to knowing the "rules" or "strategies" of trading, I am studied, and I have learned extensively about the stock market and trading within it.

Maybe, to crack this code, it took a totally disinterested person like me, an athlete, a novelist, a pencil artist, who really never liked the stock market, aside from the movie *Trading Places*, my favorite 1980s comedy . . . possibly favorite comedy of all time. (Side note: I couldn't believe it! I was walking by some shops in Los Angeles a week ago, and Jamie Lee Curtis, who starred in that very movie, was walking right down the sidewalk in front of me, I tried to say "Hi" to her, and I think I did, but she barely reacted. LOL.) Maybe it took a random guy with no grooming on the subject to see this blatantly obvious glitch. Because to me the pattern was so ridiculously apparent, I couldn't believe it was that easy.

It was like Eddie Murphy's character in the movie *Trading Places*. He came off the street as a homeless poor man and into the commodities trading market. Right away he noticed that people were betting on the price of pork bellies. He knew bacon was a luxury most low-income people could not afford around Christmas because Santa needed to come up with money for his wife's fur coat and his kid wanted the new GI Joe with the kung-fu grip. It was blatantly obvious to him that people would be buying less bacon during this time period. Meanwhile, the old, white, racist dudes whose butlers bathed and shaved them every morning were out of touch. They could not even conceive of that.

Eddie's character, Billy Ray Valentine, called it right and made the firm a massive sum because of it. The independent outsider, Billy Ray (Eddie Murphy), not groomed into status-quo-collective-biased thought, could see so much more than those drenched in the rainfall of symbols, strategies, and meanings. He employed NSBG of course. Unbiased glancing.

Just like Michael Larson of Ohio, who won the CBS game show *Press Your Luck,* who even held the record for the most ever earned on a game show for decades.

Independent, non-subconsciously-biased glancing.

In this book I will tell you the story of discovery, show you proof of my results, and outline in detail the exact steps that one could take to become a proficient 20-minute trader. This includes how to set up one's charts, how to discover a predictable pattern, how to use a trading account, advice on risk management, tips for success, and resources to help you along the journey.

It needs to be mentioned that day trading is risky and most people doing day trading lose money doing so, especially options traders. My results are not typical. Your success is not guaranteed if you learn with me or on your own. Practice first with simulated trading before putting your own money on the line, and never put important money on the line that your life really depends upon. Do not blindly follow me or anyone else.

Chapter 1
First Trading Update

It's February 8, 2023.

Trading started at 6:30 Pacific Time. This morning, I woke up at 5:16 a.m. with no alarm. Just woke up and looked at my phone to see the time. I rolled out of bed and in the darkness, found my sweatpants, slid them on quietly, put on my glasses, stuck my feet in my slippers, and carefully walked out of the room so as not to wake my lovely wife, the mother of my toddler boy, Owen.

I went straight for the Keurig. I found my mug that says "20-Minute Trader," filled the Keurig with water, put in a medium roast pod called Big Bang from Pete's Coffee, and hit the button. I went and used the restroom, and upon my return, the cup was filled to the brim with life-giving, dark brown super juice.

I went into my home office, opened up my laptop, noted some email messages and texts, responded to these, and then did my pre-market research to publish my opinions to those who want to read them.

At around 6:26 a.m., I opened my charting platform, ensured the settings were correct, and opened the trading app on my phone. I prepared my trade by selecting the stock ticker I wanted to trade on my phone's screen. Now, all I needed to do was hit the "buy" button when the chart in front of me convinced me that the stock's share price would jump up based on the criteria I had determined through previous research.

At 6:30 a.m., the market opened, and the lines on my one-second chart came to life, moving up and down rapidly. For every second the chart ticked forward in time, the lines extended, moving across the screen like fast worms. One line tracked the changing value of the stock price, and the other tracked the changing value of an index. These values go up, down, or stay the same every second. At exactly 6:35:04, those criteria I was watching for appeared, and I hit the "buy" button on my phone.

I paid exactly $58,380 to place this investment. Once I did, I saw in my digital wallet, known as a "portfolio" in the trading app I use, that I now owned the investment I purchased. It showed me that I paid $58,380 for it.

Within ten seconds, I placed an order to sell it for $59,430 so that if the value jumped that high, it would sell then and there for that price. Obediently and as predicted, the stock price rose in value by more than 20 cents, which was the amount it needed to rise for me to get my target price.

At exactly 6:36 a.m. and zero seconds, 56 seconds after I bought it, the investment item sold for $59,430, $1,050 more than I paid for it.

Why? Because when I identified the pattern criteria that told me the stock price was likely to jump upward by a small amount, I bought. Then it did jump by only 22 cents, and as a result, the items I bought became more valuable and, therefore, sold for the higher price I asked for, $1,050 more than I paid for it 56 seconds earlier. In other words, I made $1,050 from doing that trade by purchasing a stock market instrument and then selling it for higher moments later.

At 6:40 and 14 seconds, I then did a second, much smaller trade. This one profited only $48. My daily total was $1,098. The fees and commissions connected with these four trades (two buys and two sells) were $41.13. The price of doing business. Therefore, my actual daily profit was $1,098 minus $41.13, which equaled $1,056.87.

I closed my laptop and started on other tasks.

At 6:44 a.m., I took a screenshot, which you can see here, along with the comparative image of what the account value was at the beginning of the year on January 3 before any trading had begun (Figs. 1.1 and 1.2).

The screenshots of the trading account app display two important figures. They are 1) the Account Value, which shows the current balance of your account with all fees and commissions subtracted automatically, and 2) the Year-To-Date or YTD, which simply means the total profit or loss since the first day of the year,

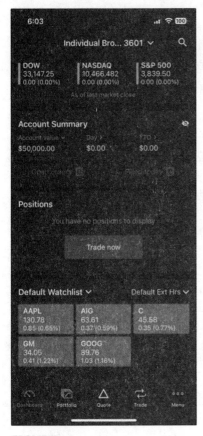

FIGURE 1.1

Jan 3

FIGURE 1.2

Feb 8

without subtracting fees and commissions. The account value says, for January 3 (the first trading day of 2023), $50,000 even, as I had funded it like that to the penny. The Year-To-Date says 0 dollars and 0 cents. This is the "before" screenshot. A little over a month later, on February 8, you'll see that the Account Value is $64,111.69 and the Year-To-Date says $14,933.

There are two ways to look at your profit, both illustrated here. I'll explain. Since the $14,933 Year-To-Date profit doesn't account for trading commissions and fees, it's actually a little misleadingly high. Commissions and fees take away a considerable chunk of your profit, so one might look at this figure and think they made more profit than they actually did. However, the Account Value figure shows the current balance of your account, with all fees and commissions automatically removed. You can use this value to calculate your actual profit. In the above screenshots, I started with $50,000, and the account value now says $64,111.69, so the actual profit is only $14,111.69. However, the profit on the YTD says $14,933, a difference of $821.31. The real figure is the lower one because that's how much money is in my account. The YTD figure is $821 higher because of commissions and fees. Each trade costs money to execute. Unfortunately, I am taxed on the higher YTD profit figure, not the lower Account Value increase figure. Oh well . . . the money is still not bad.

One can see that my profit is a gain of 28% value since the start of the year in a span of five weeks.

The way I got here is simple. I learned how to predict a tiny jump in a stock ticker. I buy just before. I sell when it hits that level, often seconds after I bought it. I do this daily.

And I'm sure you're reading this to find out HOW?

Here's the cool thing about it. I've taught this successfully to dummies who knew nothing about trading. I have screenshots and bank statements to prove my earnings, which I publish. But there is a reason that hundreds of thousands of people have signed on to learn about this method in just the last several months.

Let's get into it.

Chapter 2
Ride the Wake of the Boat

The 20-Minute Trader predicting method's simplicity is like riding the wake of a large ship. Something big is moving along, causing a little after-effect wave. One can imagine a large ship carving through the open seas and a small jet ski leaping off the wake.

We track something big moving and assume something else will move in response right after. We jump on that little after-motion, and when it works out, we make our profit.

It's a pretty intuitive strategy. A large pile of huge companies all move down, and some other companies immediately follow. A big pile of huge companies move up, and a bunch of others follow it up.

Watch for the big thing to move, expect the other one to move right after, and bet on it. It's that simple, and I cannot believe it works. But let's be clear: I had to do some deep research to get the win rate as high as I have it now and to verify better that this can be counted upon. Before I get into that, I will walk you through some simple explanations for some otherwise complicated concepts.

Chapter 3
What Is the Stock Market?

I suggest sifting through this chapter even if you are trained in this subject. Keep in mind I have now worked one-on-one with hundreds of people and indirectly with hundreds of thousands, from highly experienced traders to brand-new folks. Everyone learned from this explanation. In the case of experts, they were often dumbfounded to realize that they were unaware of some of the MOST BASIC aspects of the stock market and were thankful to understand better.

"Stock" means ownership.

If you have stock in a company it means you own part of that company.

The reason it's called "stocks" is rather funny. In England, the stock market existed hundreds of years ago right next to a meat and fish market called the "Great Stocks Market." Featured at the market was a bunch of animals held and displayed in wooden structures and also criminals placed in neck yokes, the planks with holes for the criminal's neck and limbs. These wooden structures for confining and displaying animals or criminals were known as "stocks." This is why the place where they sold fish and meat was called the "Great Stocks Market."

Meanwhile, trading occurred all around that area, with brokers and traders peddling their shares at coffee houses and the Royal

Exchange, which were next to each other, right there around the market. These blokes would go to do business and say, "I'm heading over to the Stocks Market to buy and sell shares." This is where the term *Stock Market* came from!

The word "stock" itself goes back to meaning "wood" or "tree trunk," which, of course, refers to the blocks of wood from which neck yokes are made.

So, that location is where you went to buy your wares and shares near folks in yokes.

Eventually, and because of this, the word *stock* came to mean "ownership." And all over the English-speaking world, we now call it *stocks.*

Stock market people stereotypically live agonizingly stressful lives, so I think it's rather amusing that the derivation of the title of that field comes from a torture device for criminals.

Stocks have been traded for thousands of years. Evidence of shares trading was found in pre–Roman Empire Italy and other totally disrelated parts of the world.

Stock trading is apparently a natural behavior for man. Beavers make dams, moles dig holes, birds make nests, humans trade stocks.

To obtain money a company can sell pieces of itself to people and increase the number of owners of that company, giving those new owners a chance to get paid part of that company's profits. Those owners also financially benefit from an increase in value of the company as a whole.

In the United States, the largest stock market exists, managing over $30 trillion. Stocks used to be traded with pieces of paper being carried around by people called brokers on horseback and carriages from one place to another, buying and selling shares for profits between investors and shareholders. It took place, for the most part, on the East Coast. Yes, this was the wild, wild East of stock trading.

Taking place mainly on the East Coast, stock shares back then were sold based on meetings in coffee houses and on the streets with no specific system in place. Logistics were difficult and required regulation in order to standardize the buying and selling of shares.

Brokers would help investors and shareholders trade their stock and receive commissions in the process. Finally, on May 17, 1792, a group of 24 brokers got together on a dirt road called Wall Street in a region called New York. Under a buttonwood tree, they signed the initiation papers of what is now called the New York Stock Exchange (NYSE).

At that time, it was an assembly of brokers sitting in chairs or *seats* and auctioning off their stock in a more regulated, sensible arena. Each broker had a "seat" on the New York Stock Exchange. At that time, it was an actual chair. Access to a seat on the New York Stock exchange, to allow one to be part of the trading, has been an envied position since day one when it was formed in the 1700s. To this day there are hundreds of "seats" held on the New York Stock exchange giving a broker or brokerage access to buying and selling their clients' shares to other clients or other brokers or broker-ages directly.

A *broker* is one who buys or sells on behalf of another. A *broker-age* is a collection of brokers organized into a group, company, insti-tution, or firm. The word *broker* comes from the French word *brocour*, which means someone who puts a spigot in a barrel of wine to facilitate its consumption. The *brocour* would be the one to install the spigot and pour the wine for a client, much like the stock-broker facilitates the transaction of buying or selling shares on behalf of clients to hopefully drink the wine of profits.

For a company to have its shares traded on a Stock Exchange, it must go *public* with an initial public offering (an "IPO"). This sim-ply consists of a company getting appraised by an institution then dividing itself into thousands, millions, or even billions of pieces, and then offering to sell these pieces for whatever the value of the company is divided by the number of pieces. If the company was valued at $20 million and it divided itself into 1 million pieces, each piece would be worth $20 during the initial public offering. After those pieces, called *shares,* are sold, there are now thousands of new company owners, and the old owners have a bunch of cash. This is mainly why they did this to begin with. With this cash, they can pay off the original investors, pay themselves, reinvest in the company, make it grow, make whatever shares they still have more valuable, and make the shares owned by the new shareholders more valuable.

As the new shareholders sell their shares or buy more shares, each transaction amount is displayed on what is called the *ticker*. The ticker is the last transaction price for a share or shares of a company.

If the company's share price is $20 and a single shareholder sells one of his shares for $25 to someone, the ticker will display the number $25 as the new share price. It is called a ticker because these changing share price values were on a machine that made a ticking metallic sound whenever the number changed.

There are numerous factors that cause a share price to change, but the simplicity is supply and demand in its raw form. It's like a mixture of auctioning and haggling (like someone buying a used car). People place their shares on the market to sell for a price, while others place buy orders for lower prices. They compromise one way or the other and a transaction ensues.

If ABC company sells apples to grocery stores and is growing in value as it gets more orchards and more customers, this could inspire investors to buy shares of it, with the confidence that the share price will increase in the future. If a scandal appears in the news about the orchard's use of pesticides causing health issues, people will think the company's future is in peril and try to get rid of their shares. To do so, they will have to keep lowering their prices to find buyers. If no one wants to buy the stock while sellers want to get rid of it, the price will go down.

ABC company's stock price is also influenced heavily by general stock market issues. For example, if the economy is not doing well, and unemployment is going up while the value of US Treasury Bonds increases (bonds are another way to invest where you are loaning the United States money by purchasing a "bond" with a guaranteed return of interest in a specified period of time), people will sell off their stock for the safer and more guaranteed return that US Treasury Bonds give. This is no fault of ABC company; perhaps ABC company is doing fabulously. But the general feeling toward the stock market will cause investors to pull out funds from wherever they are and re-invest them into more stable instruments. This alone will cause the ABC stock to drop in value as sellers have to lower their prices to get buyers willing to buy the stock. Supply and demand.

Just yesterday, my wife was trying to sell some barstools we didn't need on Facebook Marketplace, and no one was buying them. I told her to drop the price, and they sold immediately. If you understand this concept, you understand how the stock market prices work.

Other factors play a huge role in share price changes. Fear of a big drop in the market in general, fear of missing out on a huge rise that is predicted, data about a specific company that makes people think it is on the way up or down, and a thousand other things cause the share prices to change.

If you want to get more philosophical, we can talk about what I call "predicting predictions." Every time someone buys or sells a stock, they are *predicting* that in the future the stock price will change in their favor. But if it changes in the future, that's because the stock price will then be based on someone else's future prediction. The existing price at any moment is the exact balance of the pessimists and the optimists predicting, known in the stock world as the Bears and the Bulls. Bears think it'll go down. Bulls think it'll go up. When you buy Apple stock, it's because you are predicting that in the future the price will be higher; but it will be higher because the future person that buys the shares from you is also predicting that the stock will go even higher, which is why they bought it. So, you are predicting predictions.

Brokers facilitate these share price purchases and sells. Nowadays most trades are done electronically through automated brokerages and computerized buying and selling. This has been more and more the case since the 1990s.

There are hundreds of brokerages with seats on the stock exchanges. Each of these brokerages manage anywhere from millions to, in some cases, trillions of dollars of their client's money being used to buy pieces of ownership of other companies in an attempt to estimate which companies are going to increase in share price value and buy those company's shares. After that company's shares price goes up, people try to sell them to others for more than they bought them. Try saying all that in one breath. Reread it as needed.

Because, on average, the overall value of the Stock Exchange goes up by several percent per year, the overall value of the Stock Exchange is positive. But that does not mean that all investors profit in the stock market. Day traders have the worst record of success of anyone. A day trader is somebody who buys and sells within the day in an attempt to guess jumps or drops and play those.

There are thousands of symbols, indicators, gadgets, machines, bots, algorithms, methods, techniques, professions, experts, courses, theories, studies, and jobs connected to the stock market. The basic idea is founded upon the owning of a piece of a company and getting the losses or rewards connected with that ownership. All other things derive from that, whether severely abstract and hard to understand or simple and straightforward.

Many countries have their own Stock Exchanges. There's a London Stock Exchange, Tokyo Stock Exchange, Chinese Stock Exchange, German Stock Exchange, and dozens of others. Each of these operates similarly, and many individual stock exchanges interact with the New York Stock Exchange. The New York Stock Exchange is the largest in terms of trade volumes and quantity of dollars involved.

Again, each Stock Exchange is merely a collection of brokerages that have gotten together to create a standardized trading system. Government agencies have been formed to regulate the activities of the Stock Exchange to help protect people from getting completely wiped out financially, and to prevent criminal activities from occurring within the arena of stock trading.

There are numerous ways to trade on the Stock Exchange now. The common person can simply create an account on Robinhood or E*TRADE or some other broker platform and start buying and selling shares and their multitude of derivatives.

In the last ten years especially, there has been a massive upsurge in numbers of these at-home traders, called *retail traders*. This is due to internet and social media use bringing the ability to do this to light and the ease of trading account sign-ups through tech advances.

This has likely changed the playing field dramatically. Sadly, most people lose money in the stock market. And it could be said that the stock market has been used as a way for institutions to suck up even more money from the everyday folks across the land. Imagine a vacuum hovering over the United States, gliding along and sucking up money from the good people of this land of the free. That's what the common end result of the stock market is, unfortunately. Unless you happen to have an edge or a hack to beat the system, you had best just put your money into an index fund and never touch it. Otherwise, your chances are about 80–95% that you'll lose heaps.

That said, the stock market CAN be bested. And I believe I've got a way to do that.

Chapter 4
Trading Update

Today is Sunday, the 12th of March. Daylight saving time took away an hour last night, the dumbest continued tradition that no one I have ever known supports or enjoys.

Here's how I am doing at trading at present. So far, there have been 47 trading days for the year, and I have had 40 winning days and 7 losing days. My account is up 57.6%. The account has grown by $28,815 in 2023, using $50,000 principal.

I have dialed in my formula nicely while continuing to be a "buy signal snob," not making a move unless I am fully convinced. Account increase values are moving a lot faster than I expected! What's even more interesting is that my average daily account increase is only 0.9%. Compounded over 47 days, it's now a near 60% profit.

To comment on the climate today, two days ago, the Silicon Valley Bank collapsed after the closing bell and the whole financial world has been talking about it. We don't know what Monday will bring. Perhaps multiple bank closures, and mad withdrawals that will immobilize the world. You probably know because you're reading this a long time after the fact. But what's doubly interesting is that for this 20-Minute Trader system, I do not care as long as my

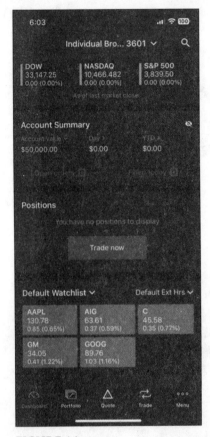

FIGURE 4.1

Jan 3

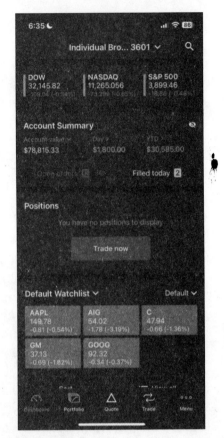

FIGURE 4.2

Mar 12

trading account stays intact. Because my system depends in no way on the market's health or lack thereof. It merely depends upon being able to predict a little itty-bitty jump once per day. And being right more often than being wrong.

Let's see how things progress!!!

Chapter 5
Trading Terms Made Easy

L et's go through some terms you will need to understand in order to carry out trading as a 20-Minute Trader. Refer back to this chapter as a glossary as needed when you encounter these words later.

While reading these, if you are new, these terms may be harder since you have not seen the trading pages of a trading platform where these terms will appear.

I will make these definitions as easy as possible, so that when you navigate a trading platform, you are familiar with some of the terminology you will encounter. However, to paint a picture for how this goes, I will provide an example of what making a trade is like. Envision this description so that you have context for the terms that follow.

It is 9:30 a.m. Eastern US time. You are sitting at a desk or table at home. In front of you is a laptop and a smartphone. On the laptop is a simple chart. At the bottom of the chart are the time values that range from 9:30 to 9:45 a.m., and the intervals between, such as 9:31, 9:32, etc. The chart's title is AAPL, the code the stock market uses to represent Apple stock. On the left side of the chart is a scale showing the price of Apple stock, ranging from $175 at the bottom and $190 at the top. In the middle of the display is a jagged line from left to right that looks like any normal graph or chart, with the line showing ups and downs, smaller and larger in value. This line represents the changing share price of Apple stock. As you watch this line, it changes, moving up and down as investors buy the stock for more or less than it was worth moments before.

On your smartphone is a display of your trading account, on which you place trades, buying or selling stock right in the app. You navigate to the page that allows you to buy stock, and you type in the Apple code "AAPL" and select how many shares you would like to buy and for what price you would like to buy them, kind of like ordering something from an online retailer. Then you send the order. It gets fulfilled and now you can see, displayed on a special page, that you own some shares of Apple. The price of Apple shares increases, and you decide to sell them. You select the shares, and are granted the option to sell them, which you select as well. Then, you send the order, which is fulfilled as someone purchases your shares. The profit obtained in this transaction is displayed to you, as is the overall account value, and the overall profit or loss that you have for the year so far. This type of account you use is called a *broker account*, a *trading account,* or a *brokerage account.*

When you navigate this account or discuss the subject, terms and symbols are used to communicate applicable concepts, and the main ones you need to know are listed and defined here.

BROKER(AGE)
> *noun*
> A financial entity that holds your money and places purchases and sales on your behalf. A broker account or a brokerage account is like a bank account in which the client's money is held for use in purchases and sales of the client's orders.

SECURITY
> *noun*
> Proofs of ownership, certificates of ownership, or titles of ownership that have a value and can be bought or sold. Stocks and bonds are securities.

BONDS

noun

Are certificates that you buy from a government, a corpora-tion, or other body that accumulate interest and mature later at a higher value than the purchase price. Bonds are a way for the government, a company, or an entity to borrow money from many individuals and pay it back later. For the person buying the bond, it's a way to have money make money as it gains interest over time, essentially loaning money for inter-est later. Securities include these instruments, and are them-selves able to be bought and sold as assets in themselves.

POSITION

noun

Each security you own is a position. A list of your securities and their status and value is your *positions*. Covered under "positions" in each item you own is such information as the original amount spent for each individual investment, the current value and the profit or loss thereby. If you owned ten shares of Apple, that would be one position. If you owned another five shares of Tesla, that would be another position.

PORTFOLIO

noun

A list of your positions, their original cost, their current value, and how they are performing in terms of profit or loss is your *portfolio*.

BUY

verb

To purchase a security.

noun

The purchase of a security. Example, "What was the share price at the buy?"

SELL

verb

To place the sale of a security you own for a price and the ensuing transfer of ownership upon payment.

noun

The action of selling a security. For example, "That sell was profitable."

BID

noun

An amount for which a buyer proposes to purchase a security, like in an auction where one offers a price. "The trader's bid was $25 for the stock share."

ASK

noun

The price at which a position is offered for sale. "Their ask was $101 for the share they want to sell."

Usage note: Both a *bid* and an *ask* are proposed transaction values for securities; however, a *bid* is from the buyer's standpoint and an *ask* is from the seller's standpoint. These values are displayed to you on your trading platform so that you can see the going prices for the security you are interested in.

Here are some sentences using some of the terms defined above to give you an idea of how they are used in the trading world.

"You could place a *bid* of $100 to *buy* a share of ABC stock through your *brokerage*. A shareholder could put up an *ask* of $101 through their *brokerage* for which to *sell* that share. No transaction ensues until you concede to the other's proposed amount or you both compromise, just as in any negotiation."

"The shareholder changes and decides to place an *ask* for the amount of your *bid*, so the transaction occurs, and you now own this *security*. If you look in your *portfolio* under *positions*, you will see the ABC stock, how much you paid for it, its current value, and the resulting profit or loss."

MID

noun

The middle point between the highest bid and the lowest ask; simply the mathematical middle between these two numbers. If a shareholder's ask is $101 per share and a buyer's bid is $99 per share, the *mid* is $100.

Usage note

Mid is used when you place an order to buy or sell. An investor who intends to buy ten shares of ABC stock looks at an order page, and listed on it is the highest bid for this security in the market and the lowest ask, as well as the *mid* between these two values. This *mid* number acts as the estimated value which the investor will spend at the moment a purchase occurs. These numbers change constantly while the market is open.

MARK

noun

Means the same as mid but is used, given your position, when estimating the current profit or loss of a security. Example: if you purchased ABC stock for $115 and the current going mid (the center value between the bid and ask) is $118, then when viewing your position on the security the word mark will be used to communicate to you, the investor, the going rate for your security. In this case, the mid is $118. Since you presently own this security, your portfolio will show a position worth $118, and in this context it will be called the mark. There will also be a column or category that says profit or loss, or P&L, which shows a profit of $3 (having purchased the stock at $115 and now valued at a mark of $118). In our example of having purchased a stock at $115 and is now currently with the mark of $118 would be plus $3.

Usage note

The difference between *mid* and *mark*: *Mid* is used to estimate the value of a security when placing a buy or sell order. *Mark* is used when viewing a position and determining its profit or loss; otherwise, they have the same meaning and are calculated the same way, the exact mathematical middle of the highest bid order (an order to buy shares) that has been placed and the lowest ask order (an order to sell shares).

SPREAD

noun

The distance between the highest bid and lowest ask. In the preceding example the highest bid for ABC stock is $99 and the lowest ask is $101, the spread is $2. This value is rarely displayed to traders, but is something that traders and investors often want to know, so they will calculate this value for themselves by rapidly observing the bid and ask and calculating the difference.

BUY ORDER

noun

An order placed through your brokerage for a security whether or not the order has gone through. It is simply the placed request to purchase that we call a *buy order*.

SELL ORDER

noun

Is an order placed through your brokerage to sell a position whether or not the order has gone through.

OPEN (ORDER)

noun

1. A buy order or a sell order which has not gone through yet.

    When you're looking at your list of orders on your trading platform, if a buy order or sell order has not yet gone through, the word *open* will be displayed on this order in your portfolio. You have placed the buy or sell order, but it has not been transacted.

2. You will sometimes see the phrase "buy to open" when you navigate the trading brokerage website or app. This means simply "to buy." When you buy a security, you are said to be "opening a position."

Usage note

"Buy to Open" and "Open Order" are two different concepts. An *open order* simply means the order has been placed but no one has acted upon it, whether you are trying to sell or to buy. *Buy to Open* means that you would be purchasing. *Buy* and *Buy to Open* mean the same thing. If someone placed a buy order, but that order has not filled yet, they could be said to have an "open order to buy to open." In this example, the word *open* has two different meanings.

CLOSE or CLOSED
> *noun*
>
> The point when the US market is done for the day, which is 4:00 p.m. Eastern Standard Time. Example: "The stock ended up 1.2% at the *close*."
>
> *verb*
>
> To sell a position or a security that you own. Some platforms refer to this as *sell to close* (the opposite of this is *buy to open*).

Usage note

"Sell to close" means the same thing as "sell," whereas market close is a totally different concept.

FILLED
> *verb*
>
> The transaction has gone through on a buy order or a sell order, and it is no longer an open order.

EXECUTED
> *verb*
>
> A buy order or sell order has been carried out. This means the same as *filled* and may appear on a notification or banner from your broker telling you that an order went through.

LIMIT
> *adjective*
>
> When placing a buy order or a sell order, the investor is asked to choose an "order type." A *limit order* is one type in which the investor states an exact lowest price for a security sale or an exact highest price for securities purchase. In other words, the broker is limited to an exact maximum amount when buying and will not spend a penny more than that to buy a security, and is limited to exact minimum amount when selling, and will not sell the security for less than that.

Usage note

If *limit* is selected, then the trader/investor is asked for the *limit price*. The brokerage will carry out the order without going lower than this limit price for the sale of a position or higher than this limit price for the purchase of the security.

Example: I decide that I want to buy Apple stock for no more than $175 per share. Its current price, when I make this choice, is $178. I place a limit order for $175 for ten shares of Apple stock. The broker makes this bid known in the pool of trades that they have access to, looking for a seller that is willing to part with their shares for $175. Perhaps there are no such sellers, in which case the order remains *open* until the price drops low enough that someone is finally willing to sell the shares for that value.

Following this, the trader places another *limit order* to sell the shares for NO LESS than $178. This trader simply selects *Limit Order* when asked for the type of order desired and is then asked for the price. This trader chooses $178. The result is that the brokerage will not sell it for less than that under any circumstances. The order remains open until the price goes high enough that someone bids $178 for the shares, and the brokerage sells them for that value.

MARKET
adjective
An order type that an investor may select in which the broker will make the transaction at the highest bid available for the sale of a position or at the lowest ask available for the purchase of a security. In essence, it will be bought or sold at the going market rate, generally to enter or exit as fast as possible.

Usage note
Limit and *market* are the two most common order types you will interact with. You will select limit orders to regulate how much you spend or how much you sell something for, so as not to lose money unnecessarily. You select *market* if you need to get in or out of a position fast and are willing to miss out on some money to do so.

COST BASIS
noun
What you paid originally for a particular security. This will appear in your portfolio when viewing a position.

INDEX
noun
A chart or a number created by a financial institution or journal to help diagnose how the general market is doing compared to earlier times. The number chosen for the index is usually a combination of the stock values of a number of companies, with an additional equation involved that allows the companies to be weighted properly in the index. Indexes represent some aspect of the stock market or the stock market as a whole and attempt to estimate its health and thereby act as an indicator by looking at whether the number is going higher or lower.

YTD (Year-To-Date)
noun
The overall profit or loss that you have from January 1 of this year to the present, on the account shown.

CALL OPTIONS
noun
See the next chapter for this one.

Chapter 6

What Is a Call Option?

Now, understanding stocks is pretty straightforward. Piece of a company. It has value. You own it for a bit, sell it for a profit, hopefully.

Well, it turns out there are another bunch of instruments that derive from stocks that also have the ability to be bought and sold for a profit or loss.

Options are just confusing enough to keep a lot of people from working with them, but they're also just easy enough that the retail trader who isn't an expert can get through the discomfort of learning what they are and potentially gain from this understanding.

Imagine you only have $1,000 to invest, and you're looking at a stock like Apple, which has a share price around $150. You do that math realizing the most you can buy is about six shares. So, if you buy those six shares and the stock goes up by $5 you would make $30. Not too amazing. But the math is straightforward.

What if I told you that you could rent 100 shares of Apple using that $1,000 and get the same profits you would get as if you owned 100 shares rather than only 6? Then, if the price went up by $5, you would make $500?

That's a bit like what call options are. Of course, if the price dropped by $5, you would also lose $500. So, you put the $1,000 in by purchasing a call option, and if the price changes by $5, you gain or lose $500. If you happen to have a great deal of certainty that the price was going to go up, then call options could be the winning lottery ticket, the golden goose, the royal flush. Otherwise, it's simply gambling, and there is a reason Las Vegas casinos are so lucrative. Gamblers lose a lot to the house.

By the way, the price changes on call options are not actually that precise, meaning it is not exactly as if you had 100 shares, but it is close enough for the rental analogy to work. This is not what is really happening, though, but the concept of how these instruments work has been best explained as similar to renting 100 shares, when I defined this to the tens of thousands of people that I have attempted to teach options.

As I break down the actual definition of call options, I want you to keep in mind that the real definition of call options does not matter nearly as much as the rental analogy that I came up with: 99.999% of those who will interact with call options buy them in hopes they will go up in price and sell them, exactly like stocks. People can buy and sell them like hot potatoes, and it doesn't matter to them what happens with the call option afterward. The real understanding of call options and their use only applies to the tiny, tiny percent of people who need to know and use the technical definition. So, as I define this technical and true definition for you, don't think that you need to do anything because of these concepts. The only thing that matters to people like us is that when we buy call options, we essentially rent a bunch of shares and hope to sell for more than the price it was purchased for. Simple as that.

What is a call option, really? It's a reservation on 100 shares of someone's stock.

If you buy a call option, this is what you are saying, "Hey you, set aside those 100 shares for me for the next couple weeks and reserve them for me to buy at a specifically named fixed price. Here's a thousand bucks for the contract that guarantees that. Okay, sign here. Great! Thanks!"

Let me point out a key element here: the fixed reservation price. This shareholder is selling you a contract that states that you can buy their 100 shares at a fixed, stated price, like a coupon. Keep that in mind as you learn more about this. Also, keep in mind this share-holder is not allowed to sell these to anyone once the contract is bought. They are on hold for the owner of the call option contract, who now has the exclusive right to buy them, hence the use of the word *option*.

Because the price of the reserved shares is fixed, if the real-time market price of that stock goes up, the value of the contract you're holding goes up as well. Because now you have the ability to buy these 100 shares for less than they are currently worth. Instant value. It's like having a contract to buy a Mercedes for a fixed price of $40,000, and then it turns out that Mercedes is now worth $70,000, but you're still guaranteed the $40,000 coupon price. Well, that contract will be worth at least $30,000, inherently.

It's right about here that the people who hated school start saying, "Call options are not for me; there's too much math. I hated math in school." But I can guarantee if you can get through understanding this little bit of math, then call options will be a breeze for you.

We will walk through the seven or eight elements and components of a call option, but I want to re-emphasize the one main thing as the guiding principle of the call option contract that applies to 99.99% of traders, and this should remain the thing that you understand about them. Because as we discuss the rest of these elements, an everyday at-home trader is likely to start wondering what they need to do with this info, and could get confused and discouraged. I want to mention this beforehand so as you hear it, you always remind yourself that the basic idea for 99.99% of traders using call options is this:

> You buy the call option when the share price of the company is at a certain price. If the share price goes up shortly after you buy it, the value of the option goes up as well. If the share price of the company goes down, the value of the call option also goes down. You can sell the call option the same way you sell stocks. You go into your portfolio in your account, select the call option you own, hit "sell" and send the order. It's now gone. And you either have more money or less money than you spent at the beginning, depending on whether the

share price goes up or down after you buy it. For the average trader,
the only difference between buying stock and buying options is that
you can make or lose a lot more money with options than you can
with stock, given the same price movements.

The goal of 99.99% of traders that buy call options is to buy it, and when the share price goes up, sell the contract for more than the purchase price. The main appeal about call options for the at-home trader is the possibility of making a lot of money while using a fairly small amount.

Unfortunately, most call options traders are losers. And I mean that literally. Not like the insult, "You're a loser." I just mean some-one who loses. They lose money. For the exact same reason that casino guests lose money, whatever that reason, but either way, most of them are losers.

As I break down the component parts of the call option, remem-ber the simplicity. People buy them by hitting "send" on an order they place on their trading app or site. Within a second or two the order fills at a specific moment, like 9:33:25 a.m. At that exact moment, the share price of the underlying stock is, for example, $159.34. If seconds, minutes, or hours later the share price of the stock moves to $159.90 (66 cents higher), the call option gains value. If the trader inspected the portfolio, there would be a gain in the value of the position. It would show a profit of around $66 (it's actu-ally a little less but I'll explain that later). If the trader sells it at that point, they profit.

I will now walk you through the several components.

It is called a "call" because this contract gives you the right to call toward you something of value. If you look up the word "call" in the dictionary, you will find many definitions, but in essence, a common denominator of the definitions is the idea "to bring some-thing to you or demand that something come to you." If you call something to mind, you bring it to your awareness. If a court calls you to testify, they bring you in through an official demand. In finance, it literally means to demand payment owed or demand the presentation of some security. You may not have heard of this usage, but "calling a loan" means "to demand payment of a loan." With a call option, you are buying the right to call another person's shares to you for an exact agreed-upon amount, in other words, to bring those shares over to you. There are 18 other definitions as well. But for this usage, that's what it means.

It is called "option" because it grants someone the choice to buy. Reserving those 100 shares for you means that you have the *option* to buy them, the choice. You can *call* for them. You have the *Option* to *Call* the shares to you for the price that was promised. This is all part of the "contract." Hence, it is a "call option contract."

Here are the four key elements of a call option contract.

First, there is the price of the underlying shares at the time of purchase. If you bought a call option for Apple stock at 9:33:25 a.m., it is important to know what the share price was at that exact moment. Apple stock could have been, for example, $159.34 at that exact moment.

The second component of the option contract is the price that you agree that the shares may be purchased for. This is called the *strike price*. This is like the coupon price for those shares—it is fixed.

The third component is the *expiry date*. This is the date that the contract expires, and the contract holder no longer retains permission to buy the shares for the strike price. Anytime between the purchase and the expiry date, the contract holder can buy those shares from the shareholder who sold the option contract for the stated strike price.

The fourth thing is that each contract represents 100 shares.

The fifth thing is the contract price. How much you will pay for this call option contract, or how much you will sell it for.

Therefore, there are three completely different prices at play here, and you must understand the difference:

The Share price.
The Strike price.
The Contract price.

Most of the time the way call options work is when the person buys the contract when the share price of the stock is at, say, $150 per share. The share price of the stock goes up to $151 per share, and the person sells the call option contract for about $100 more than they paid for it. If they only paid $500 for that contract and sold it for $600, they just made a 20% profit because a $100 profit with a $500 investment is 20%.

But in reality, when you are holding that contract under your ownership, you have the right to compel the shareholder to sell you their 100 shares for the strike price listed on the contract.

Let's walk through a brief example. You spend $1,000 to buy a contract from Bob, the shareholder, which gives you the option to purchase 100 shares of his Apple stock for $150 per share. In other words, you have the full RIGHT to pay $15,000 for his 100 shares at any time between now and the expiry date, which, in this example, is two weeks from today.

The share price of Apple is $155 at the point you purchased the Call Option. Then news comes out that the new Apple iPhone 25 will be able to fly you to the moon! The price of Apple stock goes up to $305 per share! Which means the 100 shares you are entitled to buy (if you want) are now equal to $30,500! And you are sitting here with a contract that says you can buy the shares for only $15,000. In other words, only $150 per share. That contract, at this point, is VERY VALUABLE. It is worth at least $15,500 inherently.

So, you scramble around and find a way to get $15,500; then you buy the shares from Bob. And turn around and sell them to someone else for $30,500. You made 15K on that . . . almost. Don't forget that you first paid $1,000 for that contract. So, you actually made 14K using only $1,000. It is a very unrealistic scenario to have a share price double in a week like that, but you should be able to see how it all works from this story.

The strike price was $150. The contract price is $1,000. The share price was around $155. The contract refers to 100 shares (yes, that's the standard base unit for options contracts—100 shares). Those are the three prices involved. Understand the differences.

It's right about here that learners think the strike price is the target price for the stock. Nope. It's not the target price of the stock. It is the fixed rate that you can pay for the stock, no matter what its rate is in the market. It is a coupon that allows you to buy the shares for a fixed price, regardless of the market's going rate.

The at-home trader rarely goes through all that. In the example above, you could just as easily go on to your trading app, hit sell, and make the $15K like that. So that's what happens with options trading, even though the underlying agreement has to do with this ability and option to purchase stock, and all that jazz.

Usually, you're playing hot potato with the call option contract. Get it, get rid of it. Yeah, maybe someone somewhere down the line will decide to exercise the contract and buy the shares connected with it for the existing strike price. But most of the time, they just expire worthless after changing hands throughout their lifespan, which is often only a week or two.

So, the false but easy-to-understand definition of a call option contract is:

You rent someone's shares by paying for the contract, the price changes, and you sell the contract for a higher or lower price than you paid. And the general formula is that you will get a similar price change as if you had 100 shares of that stock.

The true definition is:

A call option is a contract for a reservation of 100 shares at a specific price over a stated period of time. It gives the holder of the contract the right to buy those 100 shares for the stated strike price anytime they want to between now and the stated expiry.

In the 20-Minute Trader system, we generally hold a call option contract for less than a few minutes. We predict a jump in the stock, we buy a call option contract for, say $1,000, 30 seconds later the stock's price goes up by $0.25, and we sell the $1,000 contract for $1,025. We have now made 2.5% on that contract. Many 20-minute traders will do that but with maybe five contracts. Which means they make $125 on that one little move. And, of course, they had to use $5,000 to buy those five contracts.

2.5% of $5,000 is $125. Doing that daily for ten days—that's a fun amount of money. Of course, on average, at least one of those days could be a losing day, so the overall profit and loss wouldn't be as spectacular as ten straight wins, but it would still be pretty awesome.

While no gains are guaranteed, the above description of how a 20-Minute Trader's experience goes is not a fake example. Far from typical for a day trader, but certainly, it does happen, as can be seen on my personal updates throughout this book.

Here's a walkthrough of a Jeremy trade.

I have my laptop open with a moving chart on it. I also have my smartphone in my left hand. I open the app for my trading account.

I go to a page called "Trade." I choose the stock that I want. Let's say I choose Lululemon. I select "Call." I am asked to decide upon an expiry date and a strike price (coupon price). I glance at the going rate for the stock and note that it is around $300. I am given a choice of different strike prices (coupon prices). I choose $301, with an expiry of one week. Upon choosing this, I am presented with the current going price, which may be $1,000. I select how many contracts I want to buy, let's say five. On that trade page, it tells me that the price of my order is $5,000, just like when you go to your cart when purchasing something online. Now, I watch the chart on my laptop and see the lines moving around. I see the required criteria, and it's time to buy right now. I hit "Send Order" on my phone app. I am notified one second later that it was filled.

I go to the part of the app titled "Positions." The Luluemon Call Option appears instantly, along with the data of how much I paid for it, its current market worth, and my profit or loss.

I look at the chart on the laptop again and see the share price rise. I look back at my phone and see the contracts I bought have now gone up in value. The original cost was $1,000. That remains fixed. But now, the market considers the value of the contract to be $1,025. I look over at my current profit/loss and see that I am up $125 because each contract I own has gone up by $25, and I own five of them.

I hit "Sell." My account now shows a gain of $125.

Pretty simple concept.

Even though that is all I did, what really happened was I entered into a contract with someone I do not know to have exclusive rights over 100 shares that they set aside to buy at the fixed coupon price of $301. I then sold this contract to someone else for a higher price than I paid. And that new person now has this agreement with the original shareholder I was just in business with a moment earlier.

The chosen strike price (coupon price) has very little importance on this. No matter the strike price chosen, the value of the contract will go up or down based on the amount the share price changes from the moment of the purchase onwards.

There are some important factors in choosing a strike price, but we will cover those things later. For now, it's unimportant what the strike price number is, provided it's somewhat close to the current value of the shares.

I repeat, though, the strike price is NOT a target price you aim for, like sports betting or something. It is the coupon price for these shares, the guaranteed price for which you may purchase the shares anytime. Even if the ticker price hits the strike price, it doesn't mean it will profit more.

I hope that helps you understand call options better and how they have been or can be used.

As we progress through this book, it shall become very clear to you exactly how these instruments can be used to play a sweet, sweet tune.

Chapter 7
Five Rules I Follow

These are the rules that I created for myself so that I would be successful in my pattern trading.

My first rule: Pigs get slaughtered.

This rule came about because whenever I got greedy and tried to go off-pattern to follow something other than what I had known to be successful, nine out of ten times, I lost a nice chunk of change. Essentially the pig inside of me, the greedy pig inside, would walk me straight into the slaughterhouse. The point is, if I go off-pattern and do something that I have a hunch about or I think I'm going to be lucky and a little bit greedy, I usually discover that it is a road to failure. Sadly, this often works at first, leaving me falsely confident that it will work again when I try it. This confidence is really the warm and comforting anesthesia before the amputation.

My second rule: If I can't see it, I flee it.

That means it's morning, I've set up my trade, got my charts ready, know what I want to do, and as I'm watching the lines and the numbers on the chart, I don't quite see the pattern. Well, I simply flee it. I can't see it, I flee it, and I just don't trade that day. It's better not to risk it and just wait until the next day when I can hopefully clearly see it and actually get the profits out of it, than to take the risk of going for it when there's a good chance I either missed it or it wasn't there. If I can't see it, I flee it.

My third rule: If I fail, I bail.

Similar to the last rule, if I miscalculated and called it wrong and mistimed it, I simply pull out with a minimal loss or just a small gain rather than waiting for some profit that isn't likely to be there. The whole point of this system is that I have a predictable pattern that I have seen many times, and I know the probability of what will happen. Well, if I misjudged it and I bought but soon realized that I had not, in fact, played the pattern correctly, with the correct criteria, I bail out and pull out.

My fourth rule is: If the world looks weird today, wait to play another day.

Before every trading day, I always check three or four news sources. I look at the index that applies to the stock I trade, and I'll see if there's any news connected with it. If that index is significantly down in the pre-market, I don't trade that day. I also look up the stock I'm trading, and often, there is news about the company or even the stock itself. If there's any recent, tangible bad news about that particular company or stock, I don't trade that day because if the world looks weird today, wait to trade another day. Often, when there's bad news about a stock, investors get freaked out about what other investors might be thinking and they say, "I think other investors are probably going to pull out because of this bad news; therefore, I'm gonna pull out," and in their efforts to exit their positions, they're willing to sell off for less and therefore the stock drops. In other words, they are saying, "Buy this from me for these lower and lower amounts so I can pull my money out." That action, multiplied by thousands of investors on a particular stock, reduces its value. Oddly enough, they're all simply worried about each other and what each is thinking, and that is what's often really causing the stock to go down. So, if I see some definite and real bad news about the stock that I'm trading that day (I'm not talking about two weeks ago or something), then I don't trade. That's my rule.

My last rule: Frequently stash earnings to soothe burnings.

As you know, my initial investment amount was only about $1,200, so once I had made some money, which occurred after the first month, I pulled out about $400. The ideal situation is that everything leftover in the account is pure profit. It would be pretty satisfying to know that the money used to trade with was just profits. It gives a sense of calmness and a lack of anxiety in doing trades because one is incapable losing anything. Frequently stash earnings to soothe burnings.

Those are five rules I follow in order to succeed in trading as a 20-Minute Trader.

Chapter 8
Trading Account

Each trader must sign up for an account with a brokerage, also called a "trading account" or a "trader account."

There are dozens of brokers to choose from but to apply this strategy, the one chosen must be able to buy and sell call options easily and ideally from a phone app or a second computer or laptop.

I looked into multiple brokerages and settled on E*TRADE as my chosen broker at the time of writing. There are a few reasons for this:

> *In the last several years of trading, I noticed that a couple of E*TRADE's biggest competitor brokers had shutdowns that lasted minutes or longer right in the middle of volatile trading days. Such shutdowns can be disastrous for day traders, especially scalp traders like me. Scalping is a trading strategy in which traders profit off small price changes for a stock performed in a very short period of time, like seconds or several minutes.*

If I buy a call option and the broker app freezes, and I cannot then exit the position, I stand to lose a pretty penny. When you get up into the tens or hundreds of thousands, it's not worth the risk. E*TRADE has had a delay or two here or there but otherwise has been rugged and reliable. It also has advanced trading order types that I will teach about later, that some other brokers do not have. And of course, there are other brokers that have some better gadgets and order types that E*TRADE does not have, this will always be the case. But all in all, it has been the best one for me.

Fees are no joke. They can really add up. I calculate that I will pay over $25,000 in fees by the end of this year. I have already paid $2,200 in fees, and it is March. Let me explain how broker fees work.

When I buy a contract, they charge me 65 cents to execute the transaction. They charge another 65 cents when I sell it. If my account value is $3,000, and I buy a $1,000 contract and then sell it again for exactly $1,000, my new account value will not be $3,000. It will be $2,998.70—$1.30 less than what I had before the trade. A per-contract transaction fee of 65 cents is pretty average.

But let's look at what happens when you buy a lot of contracts like I do. Let us say my account value is $25,000. I buy 20 contracts for $1,000 each and sell them for a small profit of $1,001. I will have made $20 profit, right? My account should now say $25,020. Oh, but it doesn't. It charged me $26 for that trade—65 cents for each of the 20 contracts I bought, which is $13, and another 65 cents each when I sold—another $13. That's $26. My account value now says $24,994. I'm down 6 bucks even though I "profited."

What's worse is I am listed as having profited $20. Let's say I did this same trade repeatedly, 1,000 times. That $20 profit would be up to $20,000. Yet my account, from the fees alone, would be at $19,000, $6,000 less than my starting value!

To compound the injury, I would be taxed on the $20,000 profit and owe the IRS around $6,000 from short-term capital gains! That brings my principal down to $13,000 from where I started at $25,000. In this scenario, I've lost $12,000 all because of mismanaging fees despite doing 1,000 winning trades.

Therefore, I highly suggest that you account for the fees and commissions as you create your strategy.

It is also particularly vital that you only sign up for a cash account rather than a margin account. A cash account means that as you trade, you are not borrowing money from the brokerage to place trades but using your cash. A margin account allows you to use loans from the broker as part of the deal. In order to legally qualify for day trading a margin account, you must have at least $25,000 in it.

In a margin account, you will see that your buying power is often double or possibly as much as four times the amount that you have in there. The broker is often willing to lend you 400% of your account value. Of course, if the value of your position drops too low, they will take all of your money, every dime, rather than losing any of their own. Highly risky. Make sure to fully understand the possible outcomes when playing with a margin account.

Also, there are restrictions on how many trades you can perform in a given time period. Please read the rules for the brokerage that you have chosen, which are clearly listed and disclosed on the respective brokerage websites.

Here is a real-life example from last Tuesday. I bought 80 contracts for $835 each, totaling $66,800. I sold them 32 seconds later for $854 each for a total of $68,320. That is a difference of $1,520. The fees were $56. Would you pay $56 for $1,520? I thought so. The magnitude of profit compared to the initial starting value offsets the fees, which is also another reason I use options instead of stocks since stocks also have fees connected with trading. Options give the potential of so much more gains (and losses) than stocks with the exact same share price movements.

Some brokers offer $0 fees for their option trading services. So, if fees become prohibitively expensive, I would have to switch. Right now, the value that E*TRADE provides for the fees I am charged is worth it, including speed of execution, intuitive trading user interface, fast reactions to my requests, and almost never bugging.

After filling out everything, account setup often takes days or a week to complete since they need to verify your bank account, and if you fund it, that may take another few days.

E*TRADE comes with two apps, one called "E*TRADE" and one called "Power E*TRADE." For the purposes of my trading style, I need both, so I have them downloaded on my phone and am logged in to both with my username and password. I do my trades on my phone in the Power E*TRADE app while watching charts on my laptop.

At the time of writing, Power E*TRADE will not function as needed if you don't have at least $1,000 deposited into the account. For a cushion, I placed $1,200 into the account in case I lose a couple of bucks early on; I don't want to drop below the $1,000 floor. Without this minimum deposit, the app does not show real-time figures and values, but is delayed by 15 minutes, not workable for my system, which requires second-to-second information.

I must remind everyone that I am not a registered investment advisor; I am not telling you to go and do these things. I am publishing what I did and how to do it. I am also not telling you to sign up for E*TRADE. But I am telling you what I did. Also, I'd like to remind you never to use money allocated for life expenses, retirement, schooling, rent or mortgage, food and medicine, or anything else vital for a venture like this. It may get lost and even wiped out completely. Day trading and scalping are risky. Most day traders lose money. So, before depositing anything, ensure you are getting advice from a licensed and registered professional securities or investment advisor.

It is also key that I repeat to you that day trading carries a few other rules and restrictions, and you will need to read up on these for the brokerage you sign with. There are limits to how many trades you may perform within a given time period, and rules can vary depending on your geographical location. These limits differ based on how much you have in the account and whether you use a cash or margin account. While I would be happy to elucidate all the rules here painstakingly, I'd rather just tell you that I use a cash account, not a margin, and I don't run into restrictions. The only restriction I have is that I cannot use funds already used the same day; I must wait until the next day to use the funds again.

Chapter 9
Do's and Don'ts

I've now traded alongside a good number of people, and I wanted to go over a few things I learned while working with them on trading.

The first successful thing I found was that going over material twice or even more is highly salutary. Getting through a video course and starting over from the beginning in sequence will give you more than double the certainty of the data within. Reading a book twice has the same effect. Studies have shown that an operator or technician in any field reading a manual or a procedure and the various theories and explanations connected with them twice had *more than twice* the retention rate than someone who read it only once through. There are some schools of thought that mandate this double-study method to ensure the students manifest a significantly higher understanding and ability to apply the information they are learning. This study hack can be used in any endeavor.

Here are a few don'ts. People I was trading alongside did well or poorly or anywhere in between, and I noted that those doing the following things did poorly, one for one. What I mean is that everyone goes through their learning pains, but a number of folks just never seemed to be able to get going and succeed.

There was a particular batch of students really hard on themselves, and making silly mistakes that were cutting into their dough constantly. I decided to go deep and ask lots of questions.

I found some common demoninators between the groups of people with steady incurable failures. And surprisingly, the main issue was not low aptitude.

I found that these failing folks fell into only five categories. Let me break these down for you.

The first group all had this one situation in common: they were trying to do trading when their partner or close family member was against it. Here's the thing, though: trading in the stock market can be a horrible life experience that ruins people. One could be unproductive, stuck in front of computers all day, and worst of all, losing tons of money. Sadly, this is not only a possibility but a probability. Some who work hard and provide a service or a valuable product in their line of work might view day trading as a scummy way to make a living because rather than helping things happen in society, feeding people, teaching, fixing, or managing, they are simply betting on stuff. It could even be considered no different than gambling. And someone who gambles for money as a livelihood receives the same type of criticism.

However, it isn't true that every single person who gambles is a piece of dog poo. What about the mother of three who takes a break for a girl's trip to the casino for a day or two and plays the slots or some blackjack, and once in a while wins? There's something very exciting about that, and it's a fun break from the sometimes stressful parts of everyday life. Or the guy who heads to the casino once in a while and makes a little extra cash for sheer fun?

Few would regard these people as scummy. There are also professional poker players who are such masters of strategy, probability, and deduction that the skill resembles advanced chess, which crowns champions, entertains millions, and breeds geniuses. At this level, this is no longer just gambling; it is a sport. It's aesthetic and brilliant to behold. Hey, chess people, calm down. I am allowed to have an opinion like that if I want.

When a wife hears that her husband is getting into trading, she can and should be very concerned. The mere numbers and probabilities say that his and her hard-earned money could disappear with one click of a button. The mentality of traders can be mad. I've seen traders fall to pieces or do stupidly courageous revenge trades in a state of desperate passion that wipes out much more money than ever intended.

These are all extremely valid points, and one has every right to be concerned—100%. And should be concerned. Very.

The man whose wife wants to get into trading might warn her, tell her he doesn't agree, and dread the outcome. This applies not only to the loss of money but to the emotional stresses attendant to such activities. All of these objections are expected.

When the spouse or important person in one's life is outspokenly against the other trading, rather than just apprehensive and concerned, it becomes a very challenging atmosphere to succeed in. Dubiousness, doubt, anticipation, concern. These are not really a big deal. Directly stating that one is against their loved one doing it is where I have seen some interesting problems arise. The trader faced with this type of challenging atmosphere tends to have a few negative things happen.

They want to prove themselves right to the antagonistic partner by never losing. Having a losing trade proves that their decision to start trading was wrong and proves the antagonist right. It opens the door to failure and "I told you so's." Resisting this outcome, a day trader may choose to hold on to a losing position in the hopes it will go up rather than cutting out with a small loss at a predetermined stop point. It may work here and there, but it is also guaranteed to one day cause the demise of the day trader because there will be an instance where the position never recovers. At all, ever. And that money is gone.

They are also out of alignment with a life partner, whether a spouse, a child, or a parent, causing emotional dissonance in the, for lack of a better word, *mojo* of the trader. One is more serious and less playful, and, as it turns out, being serious about the rules is important but being emotionally serious is not.

The best athletes usually have fun doing what they love when they compete. There is a quality of playfulness and insouciance that seems to go hand-in-hand with success, and, of course, a mastery of the rules and plays, and over-the-top practice. To be clear, being very serious about the process, the rules, and the strategy is vital. But being a *serious person* internally and emotionally is the vibe I am protesting here. That is a losing attitude that was a common attribute with all traders that were in direct conflict with an important loved one about doing trading.

This best be solved before really endeavoring on this journey. And the solution is listening, gently explaining, and agreeing on boundaries. Some folks flatly consider trading to be immoral. Period. End of story. Reasoning may not work. If you are in a setting where a person you really care about is openly against this activity, just know that everyone I knew in that scenario was losing money. One person I knew who had that scene spoke to her boyfriend (who was hostile to her trading habit), resolved the issue, gained his support, and lo and behold; she started to succeed.

Also, having opposition adds stress that can throw off judgment and calmness of mind required for success in any high-motion and stressful activity.

I want to emphasize that the points of opposition had to be important people to the trader. Not just comments on social media and not even from friends and acquaintances. It really had to be someone like an intimate family member or significant other, and they had to be vocally and adamantly against the trader doing what they were doing in the stock market.

The next major factor for failing traders was trading in a distracting environment. It is a must that you have a setup that is noise-free, odor-free, motion-free, and at the right temperature. We want all our attention focused for the small amount of time we spend on this task, which is around 20 minutes in total. Cute animals, yelling kids, loud noises, or a stinky litter box are all distractions.

One could even extend this injunction to the cleanliness of the space. This could be a secret tool that psychologists may have failed to note, or at least failed to underline and place exclamations, underlines, italics, and neon lights around (although I have heard one renowned psychologist talk about this emphatically), and that is the clarity of mind that comes from cleaning up a space completely.

I was once running a team of tutors and educators working with a variety of messy students. Debra, one of the instructors, looked frazzled and dispersed, even a little panicky. She had five things to do, didn't know which one to do first, and didn't want to upset the boss by failing to get them all done. Now, if I were a psychiatrist, I may have handed her a mind-calming sedative to ease her ailment right out of the drug company handbook for better health and well-being (sarcasm). Or if I were a yoga instructor, I may have encouraged stretches and meditation. Instead, I noticed her classroom had books all over, smudges on the table, some tissues on the floor, and chairs askew. I started putting things away, throwing away rubbish, and she joined in. About four or five minutes later, the room was clean, orderly, refreshing and extroverting. She had calmed and could more easily attack the list of tasks at hand.

I also felt better. I decided that maybe we have a mini-cure for that well-known reelingness that comes with stress or too much at once.

Clean up.

I decided that this was a calming hack. I tested this on the others. They'd be frazzled, maybe just got some bad news and didn't know what to do about it, and I would help them clean up their immediate space. Same result. Plus, there are no side effects like those sedatives the doctor would have handed them. I also used it on myself. I noticed it was the last thing I ever wanted to think of doing at the moment of stress since the things in my brain were all so important that cleaning up couldn't possibly be the answer. But strangely enough, this worked like a charm. It created a calmer me, and always more than I would expect.

So, if you want to take trading to a more zen level, clean up the office or room that you are trading in. Make it clutter-free, dirt-free, odor-free, trash-free, and distraction-free. Enjoy the improved mental clarity that should ensue.

The next scenario I noted that was common to failing traders was when a non-professional was trying to use other people's money to profit for the other person. This differs from borrowing money and trading it. I've seen people trade with borrowed money with no problem. I'm talking about trying to make profits for the other person with their money, which could even be illegal. There are legal ways to set this up in joint accounts with a brokerage. But either way, the traders I worked with failed in 100% of the instances in which I observed this. This was possibly out of anxiety about using another's money. It is significantly more stressful to lose another's money than one might imagine. It is also embarrassing. Believe me, I have done it.

When I first discovered this technique of 20-Minute Trading, a close wealthy friend insisted that I trade his money. I refused a number of times, telling him I would not be able to endure losing his money. But he assured me that he was completely okay if that happened. He repeated this over and over. We set up a joint tenancy account with a brokerage, which allowed me to legally trade a combination of both our funds. I started off doing great, making money, feeling proud. Kicking butt. Then I started losing. And even though he was totally reassuring, I felt completely ashamed, embarrassed, and even sick to my stomach. I must emphasize there was not a single moment where this gentleman made me feel bad. Eventually, I went unusual on my system. I altered the rules to try to "make up" the lost funds, taking more risks so the reward could be higher. This, of course, led to more losses. Annoyingly, some of these risky moves pay off once or twice and give one the idea that they are valid means of success. Let me explain what I mean. When buying options, one could be quite leveraged, in which the tiniest motion of the stock chart results in a massive change in value of the position. Like every two cents the stock moves, the options position moves by $500, up or down. This could lead to huge instant gains . . . or losses. But I would say that strategy guarantees losing. Plus, the fees for things like that are prohibitively expensive.

I also want to stress that I believe that trading for another is possibly a successful thing that one could do. I really believe that. But I never saw it with the eight people who tried, myself included.

We all lost money, and our ability to perform seemed hampered by the added stress of using another's cash.

Therefore, I would recommend in that scenario, when friends or family try to get you to trade their money for them and make a profit for them, I suggest saying no. You can even blame me and say it's against the rules of 20-Minute Trading. But I also will say it's not my place to make such decisions for you. Of course, you may do as you like.

The next common denominator for some of those who failed over the long-term was if the person was hiding their activity from someone. Perhaps the trader was at work, getting paid by the hour, but trying to sneak in some trades on the job, looking over their shoulder hoping no one would see.

Or perhaps they were forbidden to trade by their spouse, so they do it secretly. Or worse yet, the trader uses money otherwise allocated for some purpose. Perhaps there is money set aside for their child's education, rent, or food. These uses are dishonest and lead to complexities and failure. That also correlates to the first item I discussed, having an important person who is directly against you doing the activity and how this affects performance. Open discussions, risk management, and consulting with a registered investment advisor are recommended.

The next thing I noted as a common point of failure is people who aren't normally awake at the opening of the stock market. On the West Coast, this means 6:30 a.m. Some really don't like getting up at that time. I've had a few students who simply hate waking up early, which has been a point of difficulty. Many have adjusted their schedules and have done fine.

I once had a group of 15 fellow traders who were doing 20-Minute Trading based on strategies I had published. Five of them kept trying to apply the principles they had adopted and were still failing. They did not have any of the other factors I discussed earlier, such as the opposing family member or the dishonesty, but were still not nailing it. All five were from California.

Now, if you're from another state, you're probably hating on California already since that's a favorite pastime of non-Californians. But aside from the things you may not like about Cali or its residents or other insanities, the thing they all had in common was that they didn't happily wake up before 6:30 a.m. I chose the word "happily" on purpose. Anyone can force themselves to wake up early. There is a recent, very popular invention. It's called an alarm clock.

These folks felt that waking up early specifically was painful and unpleasant. Even though they forced themselves to, they resented it. They even resented me for "making" them wake up. Especially because they would wake up, lose money, and try to go back to sleep. Doubly not fun. After identifying this common denominator, I informed them that I recommend they make enough re-organizations in their lives to achieve not even needing an alarm to wake up. I have not used an alarm in years. And I live in California. I just go to bed early and wake up early. Simple as that.

These grumpy traders were trying to squint through puffy eyes to see their charts and identify fast-moving patterns. Mistakes were common and costly. Resentment and grogginess are not the ingredients for a yummy trade.

Even though I don't feel it's valid or needed to mention this, the last most obvious issue with failures was those not following pre- scribed rules and procedures. I don't even include them in this list because I don't consider those people to be valid samples of a scien- tific test. That's like testing how a diet of only brown rice performs but eating cheeseburgers as well. That participant would be dis- qualified from the experiment. So, needless to say, if someone is trying out a method and adds variations, it would be completely unfair and untrue to say the method did or did not work.

If you have any of these factors, I suggest getting them sorted out as you progress through your studies and before using real money.

The best way to do so is through friendly communication with the close person who's against you trading, setting up your space for a distraction-free environment, declining to create your mini hedge fund for others, making a schedule that allows you to be awake at the right time and about which you are not resentful. Oh yeah, and follow prescribed rules.

Chapter 10
Trading Update

Today is March 30, 2023, and the last update I provided was March 12, 2023. At that time, I was up 57.6% and had grown by $28,815 in 2023, thus far, having started with $50,000.00 on the first day of the year.

My account is now up only 55.9%, having made $27,953.91. This is $900 lower than it was on March 12. Out of the 14 trading days between those two dates, I had record losses of 4 days out of 14. And since losing days are bigger than winning days, I'm recording a small loss over that time period.

I'm not Steph Curry, I miss the basket sometimes. Give me a break!!

As a reminder, I started with $50,000 in the account. It is now up to $77,953.91.

One thing that happens to the best of us is after patting ourselves on the back too much, we twist our shoulders and our arms get injured, which makes it harder to click the right buttons. Feeling invincible can be a bad move. That's kind of what happened in March for me!

Tomorrow is the three-month mark on my 2023 trading journey, and two things have come up that directly affect it; one for the worse and one for, hopefully, the much better. I am starting construction at my house and need a certain amount of money in my bank account to qualify for the construction loan I intend to add to my mortgage. This will require moving some cash from the trading account to the bank accounts lenders look at for such loan applications. I am considering that this trading project will complete tomorrow and that I will prepare for the next project, which is incredibly exciting.

It has to do with trading many hundreds of thousands of dollars. I'll tell you all about it in the next trading update chapter.

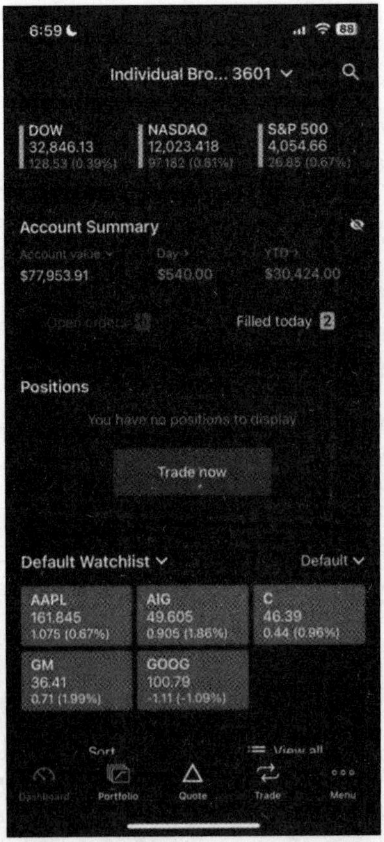

FIGURE 10.1

Chapter 11
Charts

The only charts I work consistently well with must show updated values every one-second. I also use charts with lines on them rather than candles.

The main reason is simply that I never learned candles and lines were more familiar to me in general.

As I said, I never took any courses or classes on stock or options trading, so some things I do and say may not be traditional. For example, I called charts "graphs" up until fairly recently. I posted a bunch of videos on social media, and other traders made fun of me for calling them "graphs" instead of charts. I looked into it and found that "charts" is the more correct term for this.

But if you watch some of my video courses, I'm saying the less correct term.

People can get over it, though.

Let's dive in.

There is only one platform that offers one-second charts that I could find easily available. And they charge, at time of writing, around $60 a month. It is called the *Premium Plan*. But you are in luck. I also made deals with them to get you savings going through my link! The service is called TradingView.

What's TradingView?

TradingView is a charting platform and social network used by 50 million plus traders and investors worldwide to spot opportunities across global markets. I will detail how to set up your charts so that you can employ the techniques of discovering and then playing predictable patterns.

Steps to follow:

First, sign up for an account here (if the link does not work, simply go to 20mintrader.com and hit the chat box):

https://www.tradingview.com/?aff_id=26705

Get the Premium Plan. This is the only plan that offers one-second charts. You can choose either Monthly or Annual.

Once you are done filling out your card information, you need to add "Extra Market Data."

Go to Accounts and Billing.

FIGURE 11.1

Click "Add extra market data"

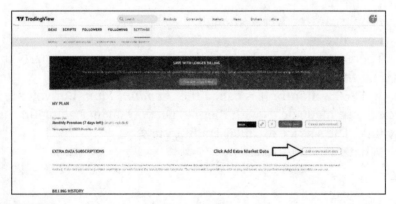

FIGURE 11.2

Put a check on the "NASDAQ STOCK MARKET" and click "Next."

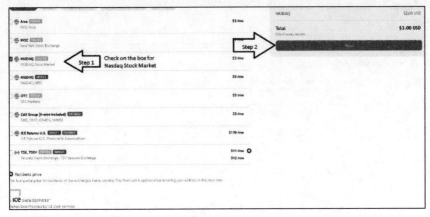

FIGURE 11.3

After confirming payment, you fill out a survey confirming that you are not a professional trader. Answer each question honestly.

Once done, you will be redirected to start setting up your charts. If not immediately taken to your charts, do the following: Click, "Products" and then "Charts+."

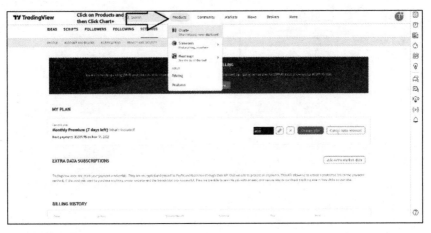

FIGURE 11.4

Once in your charts, do the following:

Step 1: Choose a Ticker.

FIGURE 11.5

Step 2: Add Index (usually this is DJI).

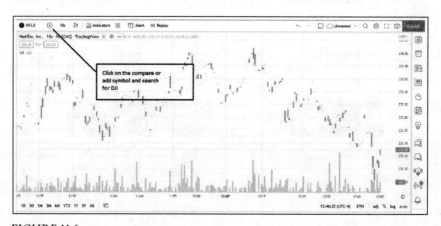

FIGURE 11.6

Step 3: Hover your mouse on the index and select "New Price Scale."

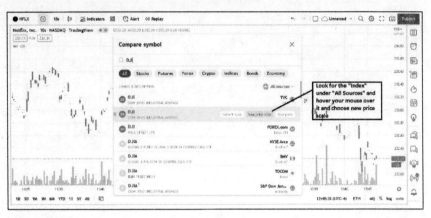

FIGURE 11.7

Step 4: Change chart type to Line.

FIGURE 11.8

Step 5: Move the index scale to the right side of the screen.

FIGURE 11.9

Step 6: Set time frame to 1-Second View.

FIGURE 11.10

Step 7: Set Regular Trading Hours to Extended Trading Hours. (If you are already on ETH, you can skip this part.)

FIGURE 11.11

Step 8: Make sure to Check Auto Fits Data to screen.

FIGURE 11.12

On both scales, right-click on where the arrows are pointed
Step 9: Rename to save your chart.

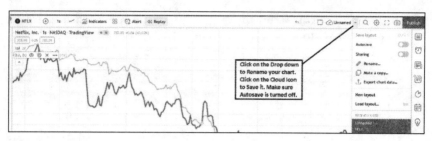

FIGURE 11.13

Turning off auto-save enables you to refresh your chart if any-thing goes wrong so that your original settings are restored. To see if anything is wrong, check the name of your chart on the upper right (to the left of the blue button "Publish"). If the word "Save" appears, this means that your settings were altered or not saved. You can just refresh your page, and your settings will be restored.

Congratulations, you have successfully set up your charts the way we do ours!

Chapter 12
The Dow Jones Industrial Average

Let's describe this particular metric, as it is the most watched and tracked index in history.

Dating back to the late 1800s, the editor of the *Wall Street Journal* at the time, Charles Dow, and his associate, Edward Jones, developed the Dow Jones Industrial Average to use as a measuring stick when trying to communicate how the stock market was doing. They took the top 12 US companies of different industries at the time and added up their share prices. The companies included The American Cotton and Oil Company, General Electric, Tennessee Coal and Iron, etc. At the time, the first index number was around 40. Nowadays, it can ride anywhere from 24,000 to 35,000. The number of companies represented on it has gone from 12 in the late 1800s to 30 companies now. Those on it now are Disney, Nike, Coca-Cola, Home Depot, Walmart, Apple, McDonald's, etc. These are the largest companies of the various industries selected for this metric. The value of the index is essentially the raw share prices of these 30 companies changed a little so they can be properly weighted and then added all together. The Dow Jones Industrial Average is the most looked-at indicator for the stock market, and it also seems to play a part in diagnosing the health of the US economy. If it is rising or falling, it tends to show how much confidence people have or don't have in these major corporations and how much spare money people have to spend on buying these shares, which can be an indicator of how people, in general, are doing financially. It has many interpretations, which help tell us how things are. Tacticians, experts, and analysts have critized the Dow Jones Index, stating that it is way too narrow, only representing 30 companies out of hundreds of thousands. Other indexes cover more companies, such as the S&P 500, which represents the 500 most high-valued publicly traded companies, and the NASDAQ composite, which represents 3,000 or so different companies. Whether or not the Dow is the best index is not the point here. We just need you to understand that the Dow is a number that updates every second and moves along, changing based on the share price changes of these 30 companies. The Dow is heavily watched and reacted to by investors worldwide. It is also the one I watch as my predictor for the buy points, the point when I decide to purchase the investment security, the call option. So, we're definitely going to get to know the Dow. However, you may find that other indices work better.

Chapter 13
Story of Discovery

Let me tell you how I discovered it.

I had just left a job I had been at for 21 years—a non-profit where I spent a great deal of time educating people for very little money. I moved to a different city, and my wife was still at the old location, wrapping up her job. We were about to set out on a new adventure in life.

I had no dwelling yet, so I was living in my brother's spare bedroom in an apartment in Pasadena, California. Due to the fairly low wages I received at the non-profit and not working for a short spell, I had accumulated a decent amount of debt. I had no job, no place to live, and nothing lined up.

I was assessing my options in life, considering my skills, opportunities, and interests.

I had some experience in carpentry and construction and considered getting work in that sector. I had also become talented at public speaking and more importantly, teaching others to get over stage fright for public speaking. So, I decided to try to write a book on the subject, thinking this may be a revenue stream of sorts. The more I studied, the more I realized that the field was both saturated with incredible gurus and also not amazingly lucrative. I'll probably still do something in that arena since my way of markedly decreasing stage fright for people who need to publicly speak was novel, and I have taught this to about 500 people over 15 years. I'd love to share this. One day.

While assessing these choices, my brother showed me a little bit about options trading. I was pretty disinterested overall since I considered day trading to be a career I thought might not be fulfilling and contributive to the world at large.

I had known nine people who were full-time day traders. One was also a Boy Scout troop leader who seemed to be doing great. But the other eight honestly seemed really stressed and unhappy.

When I was 21 years old, I met a lady named Sue who had come over to the non-profit where I was working. The first thing I noted was that she appeared to be aggravated right from the get-go. Her face was a bit flushed, and her expression was nervous like she was standing in a room where a rat got loose, standing perfectly still, eyes wide open, trying to listen for any sound of movement, kind of terrified. I mean, we spoke socially, and it was fine. But I remember at one point, she was facing the other direction, and I wanted to ask her a question, but I did not want to disturb the others in the library we were in. I tapped her shoulder lightly, and she flinched and drew in her breath sharply like I had jumped from around a corner and yelled, "boo!" She was always like this. It wasn't just one day. It was chronic.

I later found out she was a full-time trader with no other profession. I didn't think twice about this at the time to be honest.

Until later, when I met Scott, who had the exact same phenomenon. Same reddish tint on the face, like a blush when one is embarrassed, but chronic. Could have been alcohol face, but he mentioned that he never drank or did drugs, and I believed him. The ruddy complexion was a manifestation of his chronic fight-or-flight state of existence. Same twitchy nervousness. I found he, too, was a full-time day trader. This same series of curiosities appeared with six others. One man named Robert was very posh and well kept. He wore suits and styled his hair perfectly. He looked like a politician or a news anchor. Controlled movements and a million-dollar smile.

But just underneath that glass ornament exterior, he had dilated pupils and nervous twitches. A mild shake.

The only fellow that was a day trader who did not have these attributes was Barry, who spent every afternoon working as a volunteer with scouts after his trading was complete. Interesting.

I have not met every day trader in the universe; I have only met nine. But I found it curious that all but one had this same pile of qualities that seemed to be an embodiment of stress and anxiety. I couldn't help but recall the scene in *Trading Places* when Eddie Murphy and Dan Ackroyd, Billy Ray Valentine, and Louis Winthorp, respectively, were in the restroom of the commodities exchange, calmly preparing their ties and hair before the opening bell. Next to them were two gentlemen popping prescription pills, talking about their ulcers and high blood pressure.

I decided that the combination of heart-pounding stress and the lack of a valuable contribution or service to others caused these issues. I'm not a doctor, and I am not a psychologist. I'm just a person doing NSBG, Non-Subconsciously Biased Glancing, who also has an opinion.

The part about stress and anxiety should make sense to anyone. But what about this part about the "service-to-others" or this "contribution" factor? That's a whole other philosophy that I will expand on later briefly. In summary, I believe that a person's value to others, like their family, coworkers, and the world in general, is something they are cognizant of and which has an impact on their well-being. Working in this non-profit, it was evident that those who newly chipped in and made a difference helping others had a powerful resurgence of well-being personally, mentally, or spiritually, and often physically. There must be something to this phenomenon that goes beyond pure chemical physiology. Again, more comments on that later.

I want to stress that I am not making a moral judgment about people who day trade. However, I would be lying if I didn't tell you that when I had friends who were getting into day trading, I told them about the things I observed. I advised them to have a notable and tangible valuable contribution activity in their lives to flank their day-trading lifestyle. I told them about the nine people I had met who were day traders and how eight of them seemed to be more stressed out than others. One of them, Martin, had a heart attack and passed away at 45 while riding a bike.

One Friday in September 2019, my brother, Kris, was doing some trades on Tesla call options. He offered me to give it a try. He let me buy one call option contract for Tesla and let it ride the rest of the day. I had no idea what I was doing, but I watched that chart like a hawk all day. I saw it drifting up and down and up and down, but mostly up. It actually went way up in the second half of the trading session, and we made $300, having spent only $300, 100% profit! This was obviously fascinating to me, especially since I was broke as a joke. Over the course of the next couple of weeks, I learned more about how it all worked and what *options* actually were.

I was lucky that my brother had a friend named Frank, an accomplished options hobbyist trader with a mentor, who prefers anonymity, who had 30 years of experience trading in the Stock Market. We called him "Yoda." Frank was able to answer every one of my thousand questions, and those he didn't know the answers to, he got from the mentor. Over the next two months, while still trying to write a book about public speaking and reviewing job listings for construction, I learned, and I learned.

And in case you were wondering, although Frank was trading options regularly, he spent most of his time as a professional videographer and built an e-commerce store selling accessories he invented. He lacked the stress features I earlier noted among full-time day traders.

When I tried to understand the more abstract concepts connected with the stock market by reading or watching YouTube videos describing them and continued to be confused, Frank took the time to explain these to me, never asking for any compensation. He was happy to help. I am forever grateful to this friend who felt compelled to simply sit there and help me out for dozens and dozens of hours, clarifying the terms and principles that are difficult to grasp.

At no point did I study a method or strategy. This is not because I believe they are wrong, scams, or unreliable. It's because as I was looking at the market, I kept hearing stats about how people who try to trade will be losers. This was a running refrain on a loop. It reminded me of the story I told earlier, in which the traveler came upon the tribe who demonized the moaning cave nearby while suffering a drought. The traveler ignored the warnings and entered, disproving the long-held fears of the phantom-cursed cavern. I also knew that if I were to embed myself into a tradition of postulated failure, I could wind up succumbing to it.

Sidebar. I am only five foot six inches tall. When I was a junior in high school, I was five foot one inch. And I was an athlete. I had excelled in soccer when I was younger and had fast feet as a result. But basketball was the sport that mattered most at the time (in the 1990s in Los Angeles). No contest. Everyone I knew played all the time, girls and boys. Michael Jordan was on every other TV commercial and Wheaties box. Our soccer team had no cheerleaders, but there was a full-on squad for the basketball team. So, despite the fact that "everyone knows" that you have to be tall to play, I tried out for the team. I wasn't even a good shooter, by the way. Mr. Whiting, the coach, took me on with these words, "I am only bringing you on the team because you run faster than every other player, and you seem passionate. But you are the twelfth man on a 12-man team. Learn to shoot and dribble really well while we figure out a good use for you." I was the shortest player in the whole league.

It turns out he had a strategy in mind when taking me on. He used my fast feet to stick me on the opposing team's best player, preventing them from getting the ball. For the first game of the year, he prepared the team for the "box and one," a defense strategy where four players on our team covered zones that looked like a box from a top-down view. I was a free maverick, stuck on the best opposing player like a rash. My only purpose in life during my entire time on the court was to prevent possession. The first game started, and I glued myself to this star player who usually averaged 30 points a game. At first, no one passed him the ball since I was always right there. Finally, he got possession once and pulled up a jump shot, nailing it. I was determined to prevent this again. The next time someone passed him the ball, I smacked it away and gained possession. The court in front of me was wide open, so I sprinted down on my first-ever fast-break to the basket. I was running so fricking fast and hadn't practiced dribbling at full speed, so I lost control of the ball, which rolled out of bounds. What an embarrassment. I had a clean steal and a fast break, and I bumbled it. For the rest of the game, my player only scored one more basket, totaling four points for the game. And since the team so heavily depended upon his scoring, we won. The strategy worked. That evening, I spent four hours on an empty court, sprinting from one basket to the other, making layups until I could run at full throttle and still maintain control of the ball while dishing in a finger roll layup. I stopped practicing at about 11:45 p.m.

Coach Whiting told me to get really good at shooting three-pointers and free throws. He gave me an article about a guy who nailed 20,000 free throws in a row. A *Guinness Book of World Records* holder. This man preached about routine. Taking the exact same stance, exact same finger placement on the ball, and all other details. I practiced for an extra four or five hours per day after school on my three-pointers and free throws.

The rest of the season, I averaged 13 points per game from steals leading to fast breaks, I nailed the occasional three-pointer, and my free throws were almost guaranteed. Our team ran up its best record in the history of the school, advancing to the playoffs for the first time ever.

At the end of the year, the opposing coaches voted me into the "All-League" team, listing me as one of the top ten players out of hundreds, even though I wasn't even one of the top ten players on my own team! They insisted I successfully ruined their offense by guarding and stealing from their best players. They all hated but respected me. In truth, credit goes to the coach, who, as of this writing, just received an induction to the Hall of Fame for decades of dedicated contribution to the development of teamwork through coaching basketball.

The following year, I became captain and the MVP, never surpassing five foot four inches before graduating.

The moral of this story is that I make a point to break the tradition on well-worn "facts" about failing. "You can't be a successful basketball player if you are short." "You can't beat Wall Street as a newbie. You'll be steamrolled." "You need ten years of experience before you can do well in the market."

My attitude has been:

- Learn the rules of the game.
- Ignore naysayers.
- Figure out how to win by thinking outside the box.

It was with this attitude that I approached the game of trading. I was going to observe it with no preconceived ideas about how to assess or interpret the things I saw. I was going to observe, define the words and concepts, and develop my own determinations.

And what I saw in the fall of 2019, when watching charts of moving stock values and index values, was that there were times that the stock I was watching would drop and rise regularly. And once in a while, I could predict it but didn't know why.

Throughout the month of November, I watched these charts and tested my ability to determine when the stock price of tech companies would drop and rise. I noted that it made a U-shape, falling first then climbing again shortly after. I wanted to know if there was a way to figure out when it would travel back up after dropping. I asked Frank about this, and he said he had no idea but would ask the mentor. The mentor, as helpful as he was at defining elements in the stock market, repeated the old maxim that predicting the market like that was impossible, and even *thinking* that one could was a form of delusion that categorized me at best as a silly optimist and at worst as a megalomaniac. I did not resent this response but filed it away into my naysayer's comments bin along with my junk mail and empty yogurt cups while continuing to be grateful and treasure his sage explanations.

Despite his basically amateur skill level, Kris suggested I look at the Dow Jones Industrial Average chart to see if it gave a little pre-signal to the jump. "It seems like there's a correlation between the stock you are looking at and the Dow," he said.

I did and noted that once in a while, before the stock jumped up, after dropping, the Dow Jones would pre-jump. It would pop up before the stock did, then the stock pop-up would follow.

I was beginning to find an edge, a way to monetize this little prediction, and thought I could turn this into a way to make money.

I have a theory about this way of making money, and I'm going to share it, but I want you, the reader, to understand, as I said earlier, that I do not dislike, hate, or have any moral issue with someone who day trades for a living. I am merely presenting my observations. In my dealings with thousands of people through my 21-year career at a non-profit, it was rather evident that those involved with helping others genuinely and effectively seemed to have a higher love for their fellows, seemed more fulfilled, and just healthier mentally and physically. Providing a service that benefits others makes the provider and recipient feel good because they know they are valuable. For most work in this world, this element is actually present in differing quantities. If you are an accountant or bookkeeper, when you reconcile someone's transactions and add a great deal of order to disorder, you help that firm or person. When you hand it over, the person is happy about it and pays you. Both the result of providing a desired service and getting paid for it make you feel good. This basic ingredient of exchanging a valuable product or service with another for another valuable leads to a feeling of worth internally. Does that mean that everyone with a valuable job is happy? Of course not. But it does mean that I think people with a valuable job in which their personal service is valuable to others have a better chance at personal well-being than those who are not working and are not of value to others.

There are plenty of activities that are not helpful to anyone particularly, even if they do produce money as a result. Some obvious ones are scamming, stealing, and gambling. There are also some money-making schemes where one can scrape some money off a transaction by being an unnoticed "middleman." Perhaps you aren't facilitating anything; you just found a way to get something on its way somewhere and insert yourself to profit on the exchange. Or you found a loophole in banking or a credit card thing that legally allows you to make money by fiddling with the rewards and cash-back deals, buying gift cards, and using credit card rewards in some weird way to churn out some cash. Again, I am not judging someone for doing this. In fact, I think it's smart to take advantage of opportunities like credit card miles and cash-back deals. But if your entire living is based on that and you are scheming to monetize a hack as your means of livelihood, you may not get as much fulfillment as someone who consults a small business into a raging success, enhancing the lives of the beneficiaries. If this scheming method you came up with is the only source of income you have, it is possible that your estimation of your worth to this world may deplete.

This can also be taken to the extreme in the other direction. In the non-profit I worked for, there were plenty of people who were so giving, fanatically and like a martyr, I had to wonder why they felt like making amends to the world. Some of these people lived poor lifestyles despite working seven days a week in the service of others, and seemed to even reject offers of higher compensation when presented. I recall one lady who had been working for 30 years making pennies and looking rather miserable telling me that she had to live off "chimichangas from AM/PM mini mart" as that was all she could afford. Meanwhile, she basically volunteered full-time for the cause she believed in. What a heroic person she is, honestly. But when I added it up, and also noted others that took care of themselves and worked the same volunteer activities, but enjoyed a healthier lifestyle partially due to better compensation, their contributions were more significant than chimichanga lady. The simple physical energy they had from the health and proper rest they provided to themselves made their work results more efficient and productive.

Anything can be taken to extremes and become weird. For example, someone might say that a nice old lady handing out candy to kids was a nice person. But if she obsessively ran around giving every kid piles of candy, jamming them into their mouths, one might think of her as a psycho.

So, there are two extremes here. We have the martyr and the criminal at each end of the large, graduated scale. Maybe there is a better way to label these extreme ends of the scale. On the martyr side, we could say people who give *everything for nothing*. And on the criminal side of the scale, we could label it people who take *everything for nothing*.

Both, in my opinion, were lifestyles where I didn't think I would find myself happy. On the *give-everything-for-nothing* side of the scale, but not as extreme, you could have the hard-working, low-paid laborer, which I did for 20 years. This person gets a low wage for heavy effort. On the *give-nothing-for-everything* side of things but not all the way over, you might find these schemers that scrape cash off transactions. The day trader could be over to this side of the scale as well. There are also those working regular jobs that have a negative value to those around them. They get in people's way, cause confusion, and are lazy. These people are on the criminal side of the spectrum.

I think you get my point.

I believe that a small amount of maneuvering things to get a monetary advantage through investments or clever managing is both wise and healthy, and a large amount of contribution to the world with a valuable service or product is vital to personal well-being. In our current society, the way it is structured, too often the reward for contribution isn't quite enough for the quality of living most would be happy with. So many initiatives attempt to rectify this imbalance. Capitalism shrugs and says, "What can we do about it?" and socialism says we need to Robin Hood everything. Well, I don't know the perfect answer, only what I can say I have seen with my own eyes. Total selflessness didn't work. Total greed doesn't either. But a lot of selflessness and a little greed looked like the right combo.

I decided to figure out a way to make my life contributive while also being able to spend a bit of time having money make money. For decades, I had already been a very low-paid worker, and to find myself on a couch deeply in debt at 42, I was ready to flip the script, just not "*Breaking Bad*" style.

So, there I was, watching charts. Not looking for a pattern. Just watching them. Then I realized I could predict small jumps in the tech stocks that I watched with a high level of accuracy, but I didn't know why I could. Curiosity alone led me to investigate further while I played around with some other options bets in the stock market and looked into more career paths.

I lost all the money we made earlier on the Tesla call option, and even the rest I had put in was now gone. I wasn't doing well just guessing where things would go and then hoping and waiting.

By early 2020, I was really strapped for cash, running out of room on my credit cards, and trying to think of a way to get a little bit of extra dough that I so badly needed.

"I could just play those small jumps that I know how to predict and make a little extra that way," I thought. I would beat the system with the only thing I felt certain of.

And that's how the 20-Minute Trader was born.

And that's also how I discovered a pattern.

That was the beginning of 2020. And now, in the spring of 2023, I have made a good amount of money in trading with these predictable patterns and have had several million people learn about my methods. Tens of thousands take classes I developed, and dozens help me research and develop it.

Of course, a common question I get asked is, why am I teaching it at all if it works so well? Why not keep it to myself? I think the answer is obvious. I couldn't wait to tell people about it. I never guessed that people would pay to learn. That was all a surprise.

Trying to teach people to discover patterns wasn't easy at first. Because the way I discovered it was watching charts. I then found I could predict the movements. I worked backward to try to figure out why I could predict them, realized there were tendencies and trends in the chart line movements, and then tested, hypothesized, and practiced.

Lucky for you, as I went on to teach this method to so many others. I learned how to teach it to people, and herein lies the answers.

Now, let's get into how to identify a predictable pattern.

Chapter 14

Pattern Discovery How-to

The first step of discovering a predictable pattern is to set up the charts and learn to use them. By now, this should already have been done. But if not, I recommend returning to the section on setting up charts and getting those ready to go.

It is important that we use the 1-second charts, as every moment matters on this technique. For example, I did a trade last week in which I purchased a set of call options, and then sold them 12 seconds later for a profit of $1,300.

If I had 5-second charts, I would have missed that.

In reality, the value of the stock is changing as much as dozens or hundreds of times per second. But the value at any given moment is the last transaction value between seller and buyer. Therefore, on charts that update every second, we can easily know as close to instantly as possible what is really going on with this stock price.

If we must wait five seconds to discover this, it may possibly be too late. A lot can happen in five seconds, and we may miss the signal.

Once you have set up the one-second charts, you want to select a stock ticker to trade with.

The best way to choose a stock is to select a company that you think is good, has a strong future, and that you like. For example, I could choose Lululemon because I know that my wife loves these products and that it is a growing, thriving company. Some might choose Netflix since it has been dominating the entertainment-provider industry and doesn't seem to be going anywhere anytime soon. Apple might be someone else's favorite, or Meta, which hosts the world's largest social media platforms. Whatever it may be, select a large company that you like. Then go on to your web browser or an AI bot that answers all of your questions, and ask what the stock ticker symbol is for that company. For example, the stock ticker for Apple is AAPL. For Lululemon it is LULU. These ticker symbols are the designated codes for the stock exchange to identify companies or ETFs, exchange traded funds.

An *exchange traded fund* behaves exactly like a stock with its own share price and ticker symbol. It is not a company that produces a product or service; it is merely a fund that contains a basket of companies. When you purchase a share of an ETF, you are purchasing a little piece of each company in that basket. An example is SPY, which is the ticker symbol for an ETF that represents all the companies in the S&P 500 list, the top 500 most valued publicly traded companies in the United States. When buying a share of the ETF, one is investing in a fund, just as if they gave their money to a mutual fund, but instead it is a fund provided by an exchange. Therefore, it is called an exchange traded fund (ETF). Rather than having to sign up for a mutual fund, one simply needs to buy the shares of the ETF, and they now own bits of each stock in the fund. The ETF called SPY mirrors the S&P 500 index almost exactly. This is true for the other indexes as well. There is even an ETF for the Dow Jones. One may select SPY for their ticker of choice, for example. This is not a recommendation to buy, sell, or hold any securities. It is simply a ticker on which I believe a pattern can be found. What you do with this predictable pattern is up to you and your licensed advisors.

No matter the ticker you choose, whether an ETF or a company, do the following.

Take the ticker symbol you chose and plug it into a TradingView chart. Then, set the scale to five years. The bottom of the chart will show various choices, such as one day, five days, one month, three months, and so on, all the way up to forever. Click on any of these, and the value of the ticker price will be displayed to you on a chart over that span of time. Select 5y (five years) so that you can see what the share price was from five years ago to today. Change the chart from candles to lines if you have not already and if you prefer. If this overall trend of these share prices is clearly rising over that time period, even if there was a recent drop, it qualifies as a ticker that can be researched. This is because only stocks that had this quality had predictable patterns.

At the top of the charts there are choices for what intervals you would like the lines to move. You may select ten seconds for instance. This means that each line on the chart represents a ten-second span from one value to the next. The line will move another segment every ten seconds. The ideal chart is a one-second chart. This provides the type of detail we want. If you find that you try to select one-second charts and it refuses you, it means you are not subscribed to the correct plan. You need to upgrade to Premium membership, which is the highest membership, and at the time of writing is $60 per month. If this is out of your price range, have no fear. You will be granted a free one-month trial if you sign up for Premium. Ensure that you use our link for this:

```
https://www.tradingview.com/?aff_id=26705
```

There are no better deals I know of than through our link. As a reminder, to sign up for the free one-month trial, you are still required to input your credit or debit card details. However, if you cancel within 30 days, nothing is charged. After signing up, set a calendar alert for 28 or so days from the moment of sign-up, to remind you to see if you want to cancel your membership or not. After 28 days, if you decide to keep it, do nothing. If you find that it seems like a waste of money, then cancel it. Nothing to lose.

Once you have the ticker you selected and the charts at one-second intervals, hit the plus symbol on the top left of the chart, which allows you to add another set of lines to the existing chart. Add in the Dow Jones Industrial Average listed under "Indexes." It normally appears as an orange or red line, where the ticker you selected is blue as the default. All of this is covered and illustrated in the chapter on setting up your charts, but I am repeating these here so you don't have to go back and forth. Now, you have your stock/ETF line and the DJI (Dow Jones) line intertwined across the chart. If they are not in lines, you will need to change from candles to lines, which is another icon on the top row of icons.

It is now time for the research.

Scroll along and look for a U-pattern in the ticker's shape. Does the share price move down and up and down and up, with each overall down and up shape lasting between a minute and several minutes? Meaning, does the chart show a U shape that is one to several minutes long?

If the share price chart you are observing does not have the U-shape happening a few times in the first 20 minutes of the day, then you will have to select a different ticker. Go back to choosing a company, assess its five-year statistics, and get back to this point. Once you have found a stock that moves a lot and presents this U shape, it is time to see if there is a predictor somewhere that we can harness and use as our auger, our crystal ball, to know when the stock will jump up.

In Figure 14.1, you can see that there is a U-shape in the darker line (which should be blue on your chart), during the two-minute

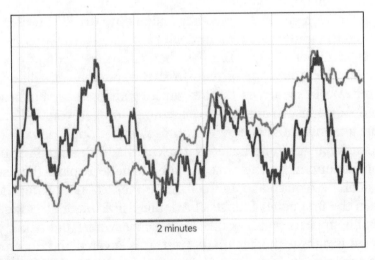

FIGURE 14.1

span indicated. Dow Jones, the lighter line (red or orange), clearly moves up divergently at the bottom of the U, and before the darker line rises.

This is a real chart of a real 20-Minute Trader® pattern.

Note that the Dow Jones predicts or even causes the darker line to jump up. In Figure 14.1, you can see this occurring in two of the U-shapes presented.

It is the very motion that is the secret to this strategy's success. You must now try to scroll back to the day before and see if the same pattern manifests. Are there U-shapes? And do any of the U-shapes have a divergent motion of the Dow Jones at the bottom of the U that foretells the follow-up rise of the stock? Look and tabulate.

Realize that TradingView deletes the one-second charts of two days before, every day, so the most you'll be able to see is one day in the past. You can see today's and yesterday's.

Look at every U-shape that occurs in the stock over a 20-minute span from market open to 20 minutes later. But let's be clear; there are small motions and large motions that we are not interested in. We do not care about the stock's small, jagged motions. I call these "teeth." And we don't care about the large 10-minute motions either. What we care about are U-shapes that are a minute or 2, maybe 3, maybe even less than a minute, but not much less.

Start at the beginning of the day, and count the "U"s that you see. There could be two; there could be seven. Look at each one and give it a number, "1, 2, 3, 4. . . ." Make a journal or spreadsheet or a notebook entry for each of these U-shapes. Next to each, describe the time span of the U, the amount of dollars and cents that it dropped and rose. Hopefully, you'll now have a collection of 5 to 10 of these tabulations over this study of two days.

The next thing to note is exactly what the index did during the rounded bottom of the U that appeared to have inspired the rise of the stock.

On the first pattern I discovered, the signal was a Dow motion of rising for 10 seconds, divergently. This means that the Dow Jones was breaking away from a synchronized relationship with the stock, jumping up on its own before the stock did the same.

For each of the U-shapes you have noted, include a description of exactly what the index did, including for how long and at what magnitude. You will see several of the U-shapes will not have a divergent Dow signal in the middle of the U. In such cases the U-shape simply happened and wasn't a result of a Dow motion. This should be noted as well.

You may also note that the Dow never made any special motion at all during the U-shapes that would have signified a follow-up rally. In other words, there was no signal from the Dow Jones before the second half of the U, before the rally. In this case, it could be best to try another index, such as the NASDAQ, the S&P 500, or even the Russell 2000, which has proven to be a nice predictor.

The Russell 2000 Index measures the performance of around 2,000 of the smallest publicly traded companies in the United States and is a popular diagnostic for these smaller companies.

Place the Russell 2000 Index on the chart in place of the Dow Jones and repeat this exercise. Go through the other indexes as needed. All we seek is some telltale motion from the index at the bottom of the U, which signifies a follow-up rally.

After this has been determined, note the values of the duration in seconds between the Index motion and the follow-up rally, the Index motion's duration, the Index motion, and the magnitude of the Index motion. An example might be that the Dow Jones traveled divergently upward, breaking away from the stock line, for ten seconds, and the magnitude of the little jump was, let's say, 15 points. Side note: Dow Jones values are measured in "points" compared to the dollars and cents in which a stock is measured.

Note all these values for each of the U-shapes you see. Go nuts on this if you want. Add details and take screenshots (this is highly recommended actually). Become a nerd if you aren't one. Become a full-on super geek during this phase. It's really fun! Especially when you start to see the recipe, the formula, the crystal ball.

Since TradingView does not allow one to go back very far (more than a day) with one-second charts, this can only be done for the current day and yesterday.

Now, if you end here, you could be in trouble. Because it is possible that you will see the beginning of the U in the stock's pattern, then see the divergent, break-away jump of the Dow, and then see the stock simply continue to fall. In this case, you are failing to predict. In fact, if you look over the full 20-minute time span (9:30–9:50 a.m.), you will see plenty of times where the stock drops, the Dow travels upward, and the stock keeps dropping.

How do we know when this is one of the times where the Dow or other index jumping is a predictor, and when this index jump is to be ignored?

That is the next phase of this research.

What I noted is that a fair degree of coordination must exist between these two lines before we can assume that a divergent index motion will result in the stock moving in response.

If every time the index moved, a moment later the stock moved as well, then our job would be done. The only thing we would have to do is watch the index, see it move up, buy the call option for the stock, watch the stock go up, and sell the call option for profit. Repeatedly. This would be way too obvious and easy. A monkey could predict the stock market.

No. There must be an indication beforehand that the stock and the index are united in motion. And how might we determine this? By seeing them intertwine across the chart, in step. Traveling together, like the double helix DNA molecule we all studied in school. Like the braids in someone's long hair.

In Figure 14.2, we see this general tendency for both lines to remain at a similar relative value. If the lines were vastly independent, then any motion from one should have no influence on the other. The two lines in Figure 14.3 show no connection, no friendship, no bond. Two lonely lines, on their own separate paths.

I would never look for a predictable pattern in this chart.

Therefore, a degree of mutual motion must exist before the divergence of the index that we seek, which suggests that if one parted the other, there could be a magnetic urge for the other to reconnect. It is this assumption that led to the predictable small jump.

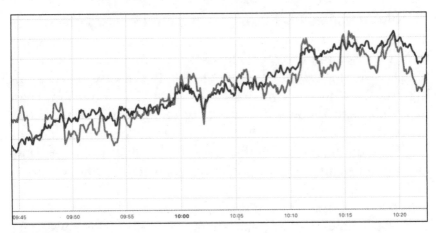

FIGURE 14.2

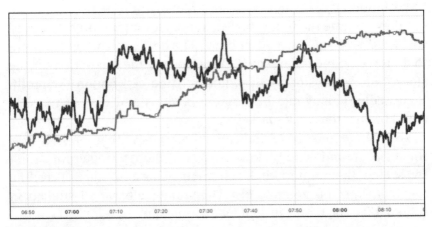

FIGURE 14.3

    I first look for a unification—synchronization of the stock and index. Then I look for the drop, which must be mutual, both dropping, forming the left side of the U. Then I look for the divergent index during which the stock is leveling out; in other words, it is dropping less sharply, and the index is rising somewhat aggressively. In these scenarios, I have found a distinct likelihood that that stock will attempt to reconnect to the index, and vice versa, the index will try to reconnect to the stock. This love that both of these lines have for one another, to swiftly rejoin and embrace one another, is a love story that has made me profit. Because it predicts a jump in the stock, I buy, and it jumps, and I sell.

So, now you must examine this on your U-study. Take your notes, and go through them looking for this element of synced behavior between these lines in love. And you shall see that it must be present before the index jump, which acts as our buy signal.

Make notes of this. Note how long the sync must be there for the signal to be effective.

The next step is the due diligence.

Go through today's one-second charts and look for times when the two lines traveled together, the index diverged, jumping up on its own, yet the stock price continued to plummet. This study is very important because it will tell you about times in the future when you see the two lines drop together, and you start to look for the divergent index jump, and see it, and buy, and yet the stock continues its downward motion. You must note all instances of these in the 20-minute period. These will be your head fakes that mess you up, the red herrings you will chase.

Okay, I will define red herring if you insist. A *red herring* is a diversion tactic formerly used by criminals trying to escape sniffing dogs on the hunt. By leaving this smoked herring somewhere, dogs will chase that, and the criminal will be free to get away. A *red herring* in our system is a false buy signal, misleading our sniffs toward a loss.

You must identify these red herrings so that you may note how often you may be fooled.

See, it is rather possible that you will come up with this genius formula to discover buy signals by studying these U-shapes, and yet get red herring-ed into the gutter of poverty.

Just studying the U-shapes could lead to a false sense of security in the method.

In Figure 14.4, this looks like a great time to buy! The stock is leveling out, the Dow Jones is popping. But sadly, here is the actual result.

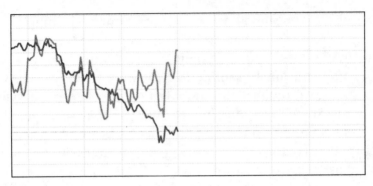

FIGURE 14.4

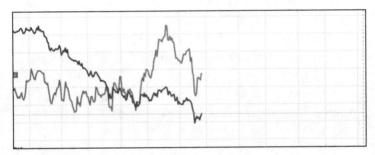

FIGURE 14.5

The stock may have tipped its hat to the index's nice rally, but then just carried on its merry way down. That small jump on the stock is not enough of a rally to even cover the fees for the options contracts!

So, a thorough study to discover the ingredients, the anatomy, of a red herring, is vital.

But you don't have enough info yet.

Here's where the real-time research comes into play. For the next 5 to 10 trading days, or more if you like (I did 20 at first), watch the charts for the first 20 minutes of the day. From beginning to end. See these movements in real time. At first, it will look like random lines wiggling across the screen. Don't give up here. Keep watching and watching and watching. NSBG style—Non-Subconsciously Biased Glancing.

I highly recommend NOT getting another's opinion about it. Don't team up on this one. Do it yourself and trust your own observations. This does not include the customer service people at my website. They are strictly trained to be able to help guide people in discovering a pattern without adding in oddities. This suggestion about not getting other people's viewpoint is not because the other person's observations or intentions are bad. It is because the system you are making here is YOUR system. You OWN the formula, have full proprietary rights to it, and the intellectual property of this formula is your possession. Also, other people's notes remove the "non-biased" part on NSBG and make you see things that you wouldn't have noticed before from the other person's bias, which could steer you way off in the wrong direction. Just look for yourself.

As the seconds, minutes, and days go by and you take notes every day on what you see, the rules of the pattern will form naturally. And you will find yourself testing your own ability to predict.

You may note that the two lines must travel in sync for at least 15 seconds downward before the buy signal is a valid one. Or that with red herrings (false buy signals), the Dow was already showing independence from the stock before the red herring by doing random things the stock was not responding to. This can tell you that the "buy signal" is likely to be false. Notice and record these rules. You must, must, must journal here. And you must go back and read your earlier entries. They will surprise you.

Once you have done this for a week or three, you will have your personal set of rules for predicting a brief stock rise. I'd like to give you a sample of a set of rules I came up with on predicting a stock rise to give you an example to work with.

I wait for the Dow and the stock to join up in a synchronized mutual downtrend that lasts at least ten seconds. I wait for the stock to level out on its drop, forming the first half of a U-shape. Then I look for the DOW to break away for ten seconds, trending upward while the stock remains lower but leveling off in trend. I place my buy order. If the stock follows the Dow upward, I create my sell order, but not sell yet. The stock rises along with the Dow. When it appears that both lines are starting to move downward together I sell. If either one is still moving upward, I hold.

I also have an exit point that I figured out based on my research: to bail out on a losing trade is a trade where the stock decides to ignore the Dow's upward motion and simply drops down.

While looking at the charts during the research phase, I tabulate what general level the stock dropped to before popping up. Let us say the stock tends to drift down by 12 cents or less before activating its rally after we see the Dow motion that we determined was a buy signal. I give myself a drop point of 13 cents from where I bought to where I sell at a loss. In other words, I buy the option based on the buy-point criteria and then note that the stock was at, say, $300.13. I ensure that I know this figure, so that when it drops to $300, I sell off at a loss. But I have that 13-cent buffer to allow the stock a chance to meander down a little before leaping upward.

This results in a decent enough win rate to make it worthwhile. But these various parameters are established by the daily tabulations I did.

When I examined the daily patterns, I noted a list of data.

1. How long did the index and the stock have to march together before I started to look for a divergent Dow motion?
2. How big did the Dow motion have to be in order to be predictive of a follow-up stock rally? How long? What specific magnitude of rise?
3. How far down did the stock tend to drift before the rally kicked in, after the divergent Dow motion occurred?
4. How high did the stock tend to go when the rally did kick in?
5. Were there any other clues that signaled when the rally should end?

After establishing the answers and tabulating them into rules, I went through and looked for times when, had I applied the rules, it would not have worked. Then I looked for clues that would point me in the direction of how to identify when these head fakes happened, when the rules would fail, or when red herrings would steer me wrong. These would then become new rules that I adopted into my set of rules. For me, if I noted that the Dow and the Stock were vastly divergent in the recent motions they made, I would conclude that a buy signal would not be safe. This is rather easy to spot. The lines are not intertwined in the recent past. Red Herring territory.

Going through a period of time of these simple assessments gave me the list of things to use for my criteria. And then sticking to these like a technician testing the method rather than a bloke trying to make dough, wound up being quite profitable.

And that, my friend, is how I was able to identify a predictable pattern in the market that I could use to profit from.

Chapter 15

Call Options — Full Explanation

An even better understanding of call options is vital in order to work with, be friends with, go into business with them.

This particular chapter has a geek meter reading of 7 out of 10, by the way. So, be ready for that. Before we start, I need to remind you that the dominating datum that you need to know about call options is that you buy them and try to sell them at a higher price. Simple as that. The mechanics of what you are buying precisely, and the underlying details of what it all means, is for your education more than for your use.

First things first, let's briefly redefine what a call option is. A call option is a contract that gives the holder the right, but not the obligation, to buy an underlying asset, such as a stock or a commodity, at a predetermined price, called the strike price, on or before a specific date, known as the expiration date.

In my last chapter on call options, I compared call options to renting 100 shares per one call option contract. Because when you buy a contract, it's like having 100 shares of the asset without owning them, and you get the approximate profit or loss connected with owning 100 shares. I also referred to the strike price as a coupon price. The strike price is not the target price that one aims for. It is a sale price for the shares. The lower the strike price is, compared to the share price, the more valuable the call option contract.

Call options deplete in value as they approach the expiry date. As the expiration date approaches, the time value of the option decreases, and the option becomes less valuable. This is known as time decay, which affects all options, not just call options.

If you bought a call option for $1,000 for Apple shares when the price was $130 per share, and the price doesn't change at all, the next day your call option would likely be worth about $950. Its value decays, which should be understandable. The further away the expiry, the more inherent value to the contract holder as there is more opportunity for the share price to rise and thus make the underlying contract that much more valuable.

Now, let's discuss how the higher the strike price, the cheaper the contract. The strike price is the coupon price at which the underlying asset can be purchased if the option to buy the 100 shares is exercised. The higher strike price makes the contract cheaper because the probability of the option being exercised is lower.

When we talk about options, we often use the terms "in the money" and "out of the money" to describe the relationship between the strike price and the current price of the underlying asset for call options.

A call option is considered "in the money" if the current price of the shares is above the strike price for a call option. For example, let's say you have a call option to buy a share of a company at a strike price of $50, but the current market share price is $60. This means the option is "in the money" because you could exercise the option and buy the share for $50, sell it on the market for $60, and make a profit of $10 per share. It is $10 "in the money"; in other words, the strike price is $10 lower than the market price.

On the other hand, an option is considered "out of the money" if the current price of the underlying shares is below the strike price for a call option. Using the same $50 strike price example, if the market price of the share was $40 instead of $60, the call option would be "out of the money" because it wouldn't make sense to exercise the option and buy the share for $50 when you could just buy it on the market for $40. It is therefore referred to as "out of the money" by $10. Inherently worthless. Just like having a coupon for a sale price that is higher than the item the coupon represents would be worthless. One might ask, "Why would I want a coupon for an item's price that is higher than the current market price?" Simple. If you, the holder of the coupon, were pretty sure the item was going to go up in value, past the coupon price, you would consider the coupon valuable. Allow me another moment to provide an analogy. Let us say that a smartphone costs $1,000. You find out that you can buy a coupon for $50 to have the right to buy a smartphone for $1,100 anytime in the next three years. Would buy that coupon? At the time of purchase, the coupon would be totally worthless. But obviously, if you believe that in three years, the smartphone will cost around $1,400, then this coupon deal is fairly wise. Notice how important the expiry date is. If the coupon expired in ten days it would be completely useless, and you would never pay $50 for it. Maybe you would pay $1, just in case an amazing smartphone appeared in the next few days that you wanted to take advantage of. You would not pay $50 for a coupon to buy a smartphone for a sale price of $1,100 when the going rate for the phone is $1,000.

If the coupon sale price was $900, it would inherently and intrinsically be worth $100. You could sell it for around that amount if you wanted to, which wouldn't be very difficult. That coupon would be said to be "in the money." The $1,100 coupon price deal would be said to be "out of the money." Both have value based on the coupon price (strike price) and the expiry date. It should be super clear how those values change based on the asset's change in value. If the phone's market cost jumped to $1,050, both coupons would be more valuable for obvious reasons.

It's worth noting that an option can also be "at the money" if the current price of the underlying asset is exactly equal to the strike price. In this case, the option has no intrinsic value.

So, to summarize, "in the money" and "out of the money" refer to the relationship between the current price of the underlying asset and the strike price of a call option. If the current price is above the strike price, the option is "in the money." If the current price is below the strike price, the option is "out of the money."

And just to mention this again, let's talk about how the further out the expiry, the more expensive the contract. This is because the longer the time until expiration, the more time there is for the underlying asset to move in favor of the option holder. Therefore, the option contract has more value, and the premium is higher.

The premium is the money that the buyer of a contract (the trader) pays the seller for the contract. The premium is determined by several factors including the current price of the underlying asset, the strike price, the time until expiration, and the volatility of the underlying asset. To provide a simple example, if the share price is $50 and the strike price is $40, the inherent value of the contract is $1,000. This is because the holder of the contract has the right to buy 100 shares for only $4,000 that are now currently worth $5,000, which equals an inherent value of $1,000 for that contract. Simple math. But the cost of the contract is not only $1,000, it is more likely $1,200. The extra $200 of the premium goes to the seller. It's purely based on them asking for you to pay that and you agreeing. This is how sellers make money selling call options contracts.

Contracts that are at the money or out of the money are purely that extra part of the premium with no inherent value. The higher the strike price, the lower the premium. Really, really high strike prices that are way out of the money can have a really low premium of like $5. These seem like great ideas except the deltas are truly awful, so profit is highly unlikely.

There are several Greek symbols that one can learn, but we will only mention the delta here. The delta is a measure of the sensitivity of the option's price to changes in the price of the underlying asset, the share price. A delta of 1 means that for every $1 change in the price of the shares, the option's price will change by $1. Conversely, a delta of 0.5 means that for every $1 change in the price of the shares, the option's price will change by $0.50.

For those really cheap contracts that expire in a few hours with a really high strike price way out of the money, the delta is very close to zero. That means no matter how much the share price goes up, the contract price doesn't go up.

But contracts that expire in months and are way in the money have deltas equal to or close to 1, meaning every penny the share price goes up, so does the option contract price—1 for 1. The simplest formula that is close to accurate is: the more expensive the contract the higher the delta.

When buying a call option, you are asked to select the expiry and the strike price. When doing so, you may notice that the proposed cost is $2,000. If you want a cheaper contract you could either raise the strike price a little or decrease the expiry a little. In either case, the price drops. Conversely, if you decrease the strike price or extend the expiry, the price goes higher.

The reason you would care to buy a higher-cost contract depends largely on their risk tolerance. You could buy many cheap contracts and profit dearly on a small jump. Or they may lose dearly on a small drop. Becoming acquainted with these various changes and their rates of variation can easily be accomplished by paper trading, which is using fake money in a simulated account. Most brokerages offer this, which is highly recommended before ever using real money.

Lastly, there is the matter of call option fees. Some brokers charge 65 cents per contract, and some charge zero. The ones that charge zero also tend to have limited order types, preventing you from having sophisticated orders that can be rather useful. So, you often get what you pay for. But you must keep these fees in mind because they can really add up. Another reason some people buy fewer but more expensive call options is to offset the fees. At this time (2023), I buy call options contracts at a price of $800 to $1,000 per contract. As a result, I pay a lot in fees but much less than if I bought lots of cheaper contracts. Make sure this factor is part of your financial management plan and is not disregarded.

Chapter 16
The Psychology of Trading

I will give you the five traits required for long-term successful trading. And I will tell you the trick I use to obtain all of these.

The correct frame of mind must exist in any field to be successful. A wise man once said that in order to be successful, the person must adopt the correct "beingness" for the part he or she will play. This coined word "beingness" is a way to summarize the identity and individual qualities that make up a person. This could be how they look, sound, behave, and the attitudes they take on.

As an example, let's say I want to be a coach of a basketball team. It could be argued that certain qualities would best be present for this operation to come off successfully. For example, I think I would want to have confidence, a willingness to issue orders, and to talk loudly enough to be heard from a distance.

Showing a flinchy, uncertain, whispery-voiced vibe might work well in a poetry reading, but on a court, it could hurt the team's confidence in me, and the members would more likely end up as a bunch of individuals doing their own thing rather than a unified team that knows what each other is doing and can expect each other to carry out duties and plays and, of course, have each other's backs.

While I will list these attributes, I will also do my best to provide a means to obtain some of these qualities more likely. It is doubtful that anyone would have disagreements with these sensible traits, but some may have difficulty cultivating them.

Here are the five most important traits for day traders:

Discipline
Patience
Risk Management
Emotional Control
Realistic Expectations

"Discipline" is the most tossed-around word in the field. People have strategies. They are heavily tempted to abandon these and try something else out of fear or greed, and they do. This temptation is never-ending. It would be like being surrounded by dripping rich European chocolate and candy for hours, with no one there to police you, but you simply must sit there and hold your ground, refusing a taste. This is what the day trader faces constantly, and of the 130 traders I have traded with personally, only one or two ever managed to fully resist all temptation with no folly. The rest had lapses, or full blown co-llapses. Collapses. My dad joke pun.

Number two is *patience*, which is also a doozie. Even I, as some-one who only trades for about 20 minutes every day, find myself waiting impatiently for 10 or 15 minutes until I find the perfect entry point. Jumping in early when the various criteria are not fully present and forcing a trade is often the cause of failure and due sim-ply to impatience. There is also the problem of revenge trading, wherein a person messes up and angrily decides to do a risky trade in reaction, often losing even more. Patience my friend, patience. Just a little patience. Yeah.

Then we have *risk management*, an analytic must for any trader. Having a well-laid plan for what to do when losing and what to do when profiting is imperative for long-term success. I had a friend go all in on a crypto coin, making $8 million in the process. He should have applied risk management because, despite this incredible suc-cess, he kept all his money invested in this one coin, the value of which evaporated like a drop of water on a hot skillet. And he was totally broke as a result.

One must have an exit strategy for when they are losing and a stash strategy for when they are winning. This is VITAL.

Emotional control is a broader category that embraces *Patience* and *Discipline* but goes even further. Notice the word "motion" is a major part of the word "emotion." It's the motions that follow emotions that can be most damaging—both good and bad. A friend of mine invested in a strategy that was really successful for months, doubling her money. The greed emotion inspired her to put a bunch more in and get her sister and parents to as well. Alas, the strategy failed much faster than it succeeded and plowed them all into the mud. It went to zero. Good emotion can be just as bad as bad emotion. Revenge trading, impulse buying, and dropping out early instead of holding if you're supposed to are almost all based on emotions rather than logic and strategy. I have even been so blinded by FOMO (fear of missing out), as I saw beautiful profitable buy signals disappear into the immediate past, that I hallucinated another entry point, fabricated by a mind that wanted to see something that wasn't there, and I bought in and lost. Looking back, I was like, W-T-F was I thinking? I wasn't, I was emotioning and then motion followed that was dumb. Simple as that.

Lastly, we have *realistic expectations*. Day traders with realistic expectations understand that consistent profitability takes time and effort. They don't expect to get rich overnight. They focus on consistent, sustainable gains rather than chasing quick profits.

And what is the solution to all of this, you ask?

I assure you the answer I am about to give is fully unique, never stated by anyone at any time before.

The only one that works for me that allows me to take on these qualities that are so vital to trading is: THE TECHNICIAN.

"You mean the movie starring Jason Stathem?"

No. That's *The Mechanic*.

"Oh, then you mean the movie starring Christian Bale!"

No, that's the *The Machinist*.

I'm talking about *The Technician*.

You need to fully become a Technician.

You have to make-believe. You have to act the part. You have to assume the identity. You have to play the role.

Here is what I mean: Imagine you are simply testing an exact strategy that clearly delineates exit and entry points. You're a researcher, divorced from any reactions to the results. An observer, calmly following the rules to see if they work or not. Then, taking a step back to see if the rules worked.

Remember when I used the word *beingness* earlier? This Technician identity is the winning one. Trust me on this; it gives you all of the above qualities. But you have to mean it and own it, even though you are pretending.

Will it get rid of your personal emotion? NO.

Will it give you natural patience? NO.

Will it give you discipline inherently? NO.

But you will manifest these qualities that literally NO ONE has inherently, except Shaolin monks, who would probably make the best traders of all time but don't seem all that interested.

These traits occur when you take on this attitude and conscious role of the Technician. You still feel impatient and greedy, but if you maintain to yourself that you are simply a Technician, then you'll perform properly to the degree that you can actually do this. Which you can.

Before the trading day begins, I say to myself, "Let's test out the pattern today. I will follow all the rules I have laid out and written down. I will enter when the buy signal appears. I will exit if it drops by $1, or rises by $1" (or whatever my stated exit points are).

Divorced from all desires or hunches, I play the role of the Technician researching and testing the pattern rules, like a lab scientist, totally fine with losing money if that is the result.

The single reason this is so important, above almost all else, is that not selling off a losing position at the correct amount but hoping and holding instead is the SOLE disease that eats the skilled trader alive, destroys their whole family, devours their crops, and burns down their house. More on this in the next chapter.

Secondly and seemingly randomly, keeping a journal does more for maintaining discipline than any other method I have ever observed. I am not Sigmund Freud or Wilhelm Wundt, but I can tell you my theory as to why this works. And believe me when I say this works; I tested it on 100 traders. Those who kept a daily journal marking their entry points, exit points, profits, losses, and other details, were FAR MORE successful than those who did not. I couldn't believe it when I looked at it. It was *the major* common denominator in success versus failure on the 20-Minute Strategy. Who would have guessed?

My theory is that it creates a systematic approach, much like the Technician factor I just described, and puts in the mindset of doing something with protocols and details. It also makes you feel better when you lose and can look back your journal and note all the times you won, dampening a desire to make it all back in one go. It can help eradicate greed when you make only a small amount. You look back in the journal, and see how many of these small amounts have added up. It quells greed and mitigates the feeling of loss, de-triggering revenge trades.

Those are my five distilled attributes for the successful trading mindset and psychology involved in day trading.

Remember that day trading is risky, and most lose money. Don't blindly follow me or anyone else, or use money you can't afford to lose.

Chapter 17

Trading Update

I t has been ten days since I started trading with $800K in an LLC account. Figure 17.1 shows the account's value on May 15, and Figure 17.2 shows what it is now on May 25. The increase is $26,689.51. This is a profit of 3.3% over ten days, during which there were nine trading days. Nerves have gone wild, I will admit. Trading at this level is a whole other dimension. What I found interesting is that the broker's fulfillment of orders seems to lag when I use more than 500 contracts. The order may sit for ten or so seconds before actually filling, which is too long for my strategy to be successful. Therefore, I have to limit my trades to 500 contracts rather than 800, which I would have preferred.

Using this much money shows that I could generate in nine days what it took me to generate in three months using a smaller amount.

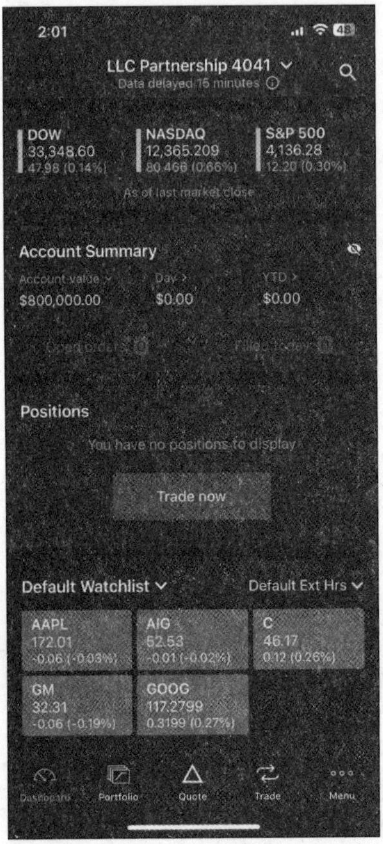

FIGURE 17.1

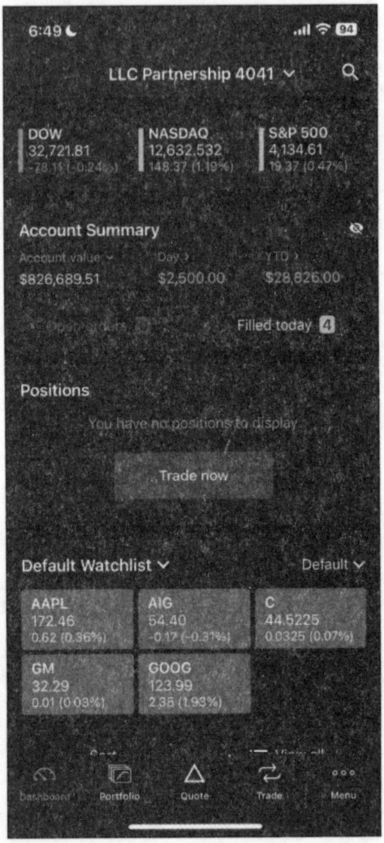

FIGURE 17.2

Chapter 18
The Bulletproof Strategy

Losing money sucks!! But being a good loser is the ONLY WAY to succeed in ANY trading strategy you adopt.

Let me explain and share my bulletproof solution with you.

Now, if you lose at day trading and you are reading this right now, in one way you're very not unique and in another way you are very unique. Estimates show that over 90% of day traders have less money in their account than they put in. In this regard you are not unique. But very few of these losers admit it. That you do and can, would make you VERY unique.

You hear about these great winners who show how they made a bunch of money day trading; it almost makes you feel like everyone does or can. But that simply isn't the case.

I happen to be one of the small percent that makes money day trading, but that was definitely not always the case.

What I learned is the *ability to lose money properly* is the major factor in day trading because the hardest thing one can do is sell off a losing position and then watch it go right back up again.

This one phenomenon is MAJORLY *the reason* day traders hope and hold on a losing position, the biggest cause of money loss for day traders.

Let's learn about this disease and then get the cure.

Don't be a dupe or a zombie.

The stock market can have a hypnotic effect on its players, inescapable unless immunized.

One hundred percent of my trader friends have experienced a particular sequence. They buy something, it goes down, so they bail per their rules. Immediately after, the stock goes up vertical enough to look like a middle finger . . . meaning they would not have lost any money if they held on and didn't sell at the loss. This happens repeatedly.

One day, the trader says, "I'm going to hang in there and not sell it off when it's down." Even though the rule says to cut their losses, they should. This works splendidly, and the trader realizes that they don't have to lose money by bailing when it drops anymore. "F#*% the rules," they say. It works again, reaffirming the conclusion.

Several more wins make the trader feel invincible, who is by now compounding their investment with winnings. Strutting. This feeling is euphoric . . . and this euphoria is the anesthesia before the amputation they are about to experience. This can even work for two or three months straight. This time period could be called the marination period, as their body's meat is being prepared for a feast. One fine day they feel extra bold and put in a lot more; the stock crashes. Supported by the new conclusion that "bailing is unnecessary," the cocky trader holds and hopes. The stock plunges into the Mariana Trench, the deepest part of the ocean.

The trader loses 90% of their account value, often by trying to throw in more money at lower points to recover some of the losses and hoping for a rebound . . . that doesn't show up.

Pay attention for the solution.

"How do I protect myself from this?"

When you repeatedly sell off a position at a loss and find that it comes right back up, you get very shy about doing it. It's almost as if it was designed that way. If someone can conquer this phenomenon and force the day trader to sell at the designated drop marker *whenever* it happens, that person holds the key to the psychology miracle that can save the butts of many day traders. Because this *IS* their bane.

Often, their chosen strategy works well if followed. It's convincing oneself to follow it and not break it, specifically on the point of selling at a loss, that makes it difficult. I once set a group of day traders on a mission to follow their own rules perfectly for one month. And I told them I would pay them a reward if they did so. This included that they would need to sell off the position at a loss of a specific amount if it ever presented itself. The reward was substantial.

Of the 20 traders set up set on doing this, within the first two weeks, 15 had disqualified themselves by breaking the rules. Of the 5 remaining, I called them every morning before market open and reminded them to follow the rules. One of them still managed to forfeit any chance of reward by breaking the rules. The other 4 completed the month successfully following the rules. All 4 of them were quite profitable.

If there is a way to create a reward-based system for selling off your position at a loss when you're supposed to, then you will have conquered this enigma. Because when you know you have a nine out of ten chance that the share price or position will rise back up and not be a loss, it's nearly impossible to sell off a losing position. I had to bribe and threaten people to follow their rules, and they were only able to do so perfectly for four weeks.

I make sure to communicate this phenomenon in detail with any fellow traders that might be vulnerable to it. But I also chant this one datum at them as much as possible:

If you ever hope and hold ONCE, then . . . one day . . . you will wipe yourself out.

If you ever do it once, even if successful, you will 100%, one day, wipe yourself out. It's inevitable. So, you must never do it. You must look forward to bailing at a loss because every time you do that, you guarantee safety and strength.

Every day, you must tell yourself before the trading day, "I hope I bail out at a loss today so I can prove how badass and disciplined I am." Want it. Create that want internally.

And happily bail at the designated drop marker. Oh yeah. Make sure to have the designated drop marker as well! Not vague. Exact. But this still doesn't fully answer the question of how to solve the issue because what if this little personal pep talk I am giving you now doesn't work? I'm sure as you read this you are telling yourself, "I can do this!! I got this!! He's right!! Of course, I will bail at the designated marker for exiting at a loss. It's so sensible." Indeed, right now as you read this, in a relaxed setting, the answer is so clear. But like I said in my psychology chapter, the temptations when actually trading are so powerful, these can subdue logic like a jiu-jitsu master can do a chokehold. When you are in the moment, sitting there with a negative P and L on your position, knowing that there is a nine out of ten chance it will return and give you profit, the ability to sell it off and resist holding on for one more moment is almost non-existent. That ability is the weaker power in that moment. Yet this alone is the ability that makes or breaks the trader with a decent strategy. This phenomenon ALONE will determine your long-term success or failure. PERIOD. END OF STORY.

Once again, if you ever get tempted once to hope and hold when you should have bailed, just once, then one day you're wiped out. But, I have a solution.

There are two solutions actually. The first is the Stop loss, and the second is the stash.

Stash away winnings to a point where you have removed your principal investment, and even some profit. So, when you do screw up, you can't lose any of what you invested, because it is not there to be lost. It is back in your bank account. We'll talk about this more later. Let's talk about stop losses. I have been through every scenario you can imagine on day trading. I have even doubled, tripled my money, over the span of just weeks and then wiped it all out in one stupid trade.

One time, I made $30,000 slowly over the span of three months and lost $25,000 in a one-hour trade simply because I refused to bail at a small loss but instead held and *hoped* into the gutter.

Then, I did what other traders do when they lose. I looked in the mirror and called myself a gambler, a loser, a weakling, an idiot, a

criminally irresponsible psycho, and a coward. The reason we traders do that is because we know from the past that we're supposed to
limit our losses by *exiting on small losses*. We even have exact exit
points we must follow. But we tend to regret those small losses
because, so often, the value of our position goes up after we sell it
off at the small loss, as I just described. But what I will say is that
I finally found the solution. And it does not require self-whippings,
shaming, or self-guilt activities.

It simply requires stop losses. Instead of trying to force yourself
to have the discipline to sell at a loss, the only discipline you have to
force yourself to have is to *place* the stop loss.

There are many ways to do stop losses, but I will cover the three
I've most used:

> *The first and easiest one is often called "stop on quote," which simply
> means that when the position drops to a certain value, the brokerage
> will sell the position for as close to that value as possible.*

A simple example of that would be a stock that is valued at
$100 with a *stop on quote* setting of $99; when the stock drops to $99
the brokerage sells it for very close to $99.

This is the simplest and most common form of the stop loss.
Each brokerage and trading platform will have its own way of presenting this type of stop loss, and it's important to learn the individual steps to place a stop loss order on a position in your broker
account.

The next type of stop loss order is the "OCO," which stands for
"One Cancels the Other." These order types allow one to place two
orders at the same time, one which is an order that fills if the position goes up to a certain point, grabbing profit, while also having a
stop loss in place so that if the position drops, it will be "stopped
out" before dropping too much lower. Whichever direction the
stock decides to go it will either fill at the higher level or the lower
level, unless these levels have been placed so distantly that the position just rides in the middle forever, which could also happen.

The next stop loss order type is called a "trailing stop." These are
identical to stop loss orders, but the value at which the position will

be stopped out at on a drop keeps going up as the position's value goes up. There is always a set quantity or percentage that a trailing stop is set for. It trails behind the value of the position, never dropping, only getting pulled higher. So once the position finally decides to fall a bit, it sells it off. This also provides a safety net while allowing the position to rise and rise and rise while the stop loss simply rises along with it, like a tether pulling it up. Imagine you are driving up a hill with a tether or chain on the back of your car that is ten feet long. Attached to the end of the tether is a big barrier on wheels that can never roll backward, only forward. As you drive up the hill, you pull it along behind you. Your car starts to slide backward, and drifts about five feet back down. The tether goes loose, but the barrier remains in place; it doesn't roll backward because its wheels are locked unless they are rolling forward. Due to rolling downhill a bit, the wall is now five instead of ten feet from the back of your car. You keep moving upward, and the tether tightens and pulls the wall behind you. This keeps going until you finally skid backward ten feet, and crash into the barrier, which is, of course, better than tumbling all the way down the hill. This non-reversing wall thing is the trailing stop. The trailing stop value in this example is the length of the tether, ten feet.

In stocks, it could be ten cents, ten dollars, or whatever you choose. The stock price is the car. The trailing stop is the tether with the moving barrier that is riding on one-direction wheels.

When you see mountain climbers attaching their ropes to clips fixed into the side of the mountain as they climb, this is a trailing stop. If they fall, they can only fall so far, but they can progress upward as much as they like.

Now, I'll tell you the best method for me.

My best method has been the OCO. This is because by producing or creating a limit order on the top, often called the "tale profit," I guarantee a certain positive return if it goes up to that level. Whereas, if I use a trailing stop, the stock or position could drop fast and punch through the stop loss pretty far and steal some of my profit. This phenomenon is called "slippage." In the example of the moving barrier attached by tether to the back of your car, imagine if the skid hits the barrier and jars it back down a bit due to the force of the car hitting it. This is slippage. And this actually occurs with any type of stop loss in the stock market.

This means that when a stop loss order activates, and the position must be sold, the brokerage will sell it for as close to that stop-loss value as possible but will almost always sell it for lower than the value of the stop loss. In fact, whenever you place a stop loss order on your trading account, a warning appears before you can hit "send." It tells you that it will likely not sell at the desired price, but will sell lower than you want it to.

In the example of the stop loss placed at $99, it is very likely the shares will sell at around $98.95, five cents lower than desired. This is a "slippage" of five cents. The main purpose of this chapter is to tell you that the mantra I've created for myself and helped cure me of the illness of huge, massive losses on one bad trade, is as follows:

"If I don't place a stop loss on every trade, then one day I will lose everything."

This means that if I do any single individual trade without a stop loss, I might as well just kiss my account goodbye. Because one day I will lose everything. Stop loss on every trade unless it profits so fast that you don't even have time and just sell it off before you need a stop loss. This occurs for me frequently with my 20-Minute Trader method. I buy a pile of call option contracts once I see the buy signal. By the time it populates in my positions, the underlying stock has jumped up significantly immediately after I bought. The profit and loss shown on my position is already nicely up. The amount of time it takes to create an OCO order is double or triple the amount of time it takes to simply sell off a security. So, rather than doing so, I often just sell it at its existing profit level.

Unfortunately, saying this exception in this chapter gives you an "out" on creating a stop loss. It enables the would-be rule-violator to "accidentally" not place a stop loss and opens the door to cascading money out of your trading account. But I would be lying if I did not communicate what I actually do. Other than instant profit taking, stop losses must be placed.

The key here is that rather than focusing on my supposed lack of discipline, cowardice, weakness, the exorcism of gambler demons, etc., all I need to focus on is making sure I place stop losses on every trade. If I'm not doing that, then I will lose everything one day. Fact. I've learned that the hard way by losing hundreds of thousands of dollars simply because I didn't put a stop loss on every trade. Now, I need only focus on the discipline of placing stop losses, rather than on self-denigrating statements and conclusions after losing a ton. The sting of losing a little is so much easier to withstand compared to the mauling of a large loss.

So, if I am ever talking to a day trader and find out they aren't using stop losses, I tell them it is my prediction that they are going to wipe out everything one day.

There is a problem with stop losses. There has been a popular theory going around that stop losses appear as orders to the institutional traders of the world, who have the ability to move the share price up or down in varying amounts in order to wipe out stop losses and claim profit. Some gurus warn against this and stopped playing stop losses for that reason only, and use a manual or a mental stop loss instead. This means they wait for a target price to appear and then exit manually by selling off the position by hand, rather than with a stop loss in place.

Let me describe the scenario that these gurus are trying to avoid. If I bought shares for ABC company at $100 per share, and I placed a stop loss at $99, and let us say that many others did the same, the institutional jerk face would see these and drop the share price to $98.95, buy up the stop losses, and then raise the overall share price to gain the profit. How do they do this?

Keep in mind that the ticker price that shows the ever-changing share price is always showing the last transaction values for any buy or sell. So, if the current ticker price showed $100 even, I could place a share price sell for $99.99, and someone is likely to buy it. Then I ladder it down one or a few cents at a time until it hits $99 simply by selling the shares for less and less and less. This is what the institutional folks do to try to manipulate the prices in the direction they want them to go. This has some workability obviously, so one could be victimized by this phenomenon. I would say the smaller cap stocks are more prone to this.

Small-cap stocks, also known as small-capitalization stocks or simply small caps, refer to stocks issued by companies with relatively small market capitalizations. Market capitalization, or market cap, is calculated by multiplying the number of a company's outstanding shares by the current market price of a single share.

While there is no universally agreed-upon definition, small-cap stocks are typically associated with companies that have a market capitalization within a certain range. Different financial institutions or analysts may define small caps differently, but here is a general guideline:

1. Micro-cap stocks: Generally, companies with a market capitalization below $300 million are considered micro-cap stocks. These are the smallest of the small-cap stocks and often represent early-stage companies or those with limited market presence.
2. Small-cap stocks: This category typically includes companies with market capitalizations between $300 million and $2 billion. Small-cap stocks are generally more established than micro-caps, but they may still be in the early growth stages or operate in niche markets.
3. Mid-cap stocks: While not small caps, mid-cap stocks are worth mentioning for context. These stocks represent companies with market capitalizations between $2 billion and $10 billion. Mid-cap companies are often in a transitional phase, with a balance between growth potential and stability.

The market capitalization ranges mentioned are subjective and may vary depending on the source, the specific investment strategy, or the time period being referenced. Small-cap stocks are generally considered riskier investments compared to large-cap stocks—companies with larger market capitalizations. They may offer higher growth potential but can also be more volatile and susceptible to market fluctuations.

But my take is this. A little retail investor like me doesn't really have to worry about this as much. I believe that penny stocks are easily victimized by the institutional manipulation tactic I described. I tend to use such large-cap companies for my trades, that even if I was using $10 or $20 million for my trades with stop losses, I would still not sound any alarms to these institutional folks trying to grab my stop losses. One of the gurus that said that he never does stop losses anymore plays with large amounts of money on penny stocks. In this arena, he is a whale. He would definitely stand out and be a target. Since I trade things like Apple, Amazon, Microsoft, and other such massive companies, unless I am wielding billions, I am just a drop in the bucket, and I doubt I would ever attract these institutional villains.

What I do have to worry about is my personal self-discipline in selling off a losing position. I've never known a single person to conquer this with manual self-decided selling of a losing position, mental stop losses. Perhaps these enigmatic superhumans exist. Perhaps they are from the same planet as Mr. Spock, and they are not affected by emotions. I have yet to meet this person.

So, I am going to use stop losses. Also, I use options rather than stocks for my trading method, so I don't think this has the same effect as this phenomenon would with shares of stocks. This is my personal opinion, not based on any expert testimonial.

The next question to ask oneself is, how can I be sure that I will place these stop losses when I am trading? The only solid answer that I know of is accountability.

Some people pride themselves on not breaking promises they have made. As a result, they earn trust and goodwill from others, and they bring a higher sense of order and well-being to their family and friends.

But, at the same time, these promise keepers are almost all scandalously bad promise breakers. Yes, you heard right, even the most trustworthy person, who never breaks their promise, ever, actually does all the time. Why do I say this?

Because they break them to themselves. Easily and without remorse.

"I promise I will only eat 1,500 calories per day."

"I promise I will exercise every single day."

"I promise I will go to bed on time." Etc., etc., etc. Yeah, right.

Sitting there telling yourself to have self-discipline actually has some workability, until it doesn't. I gave up on this flimsy-ass tool a long time ago. And yes, I still promise myself that I will do things, and it does help me, but it has very little guarantee. There are very few consequences to breaking a promise to yourself. But breaking a promise to another? With a legitimate penalty associated with it? That's a whole other story. One broken promise, even if small, can destroy an entire career, friendship, or relationship, even if it is years in the making with never faltering all those years.

Imagine if your friend promised you they would not have a party when they house-sat for you, but then they did. It would be really hard to trust this friend as much ever again. This friend has lost a sizable chunk of your goodwill and potential contribution to their lives.

Breaking a promise to someone important to you is not something anyone ever wants to do. Period.

I bring this up because if there is accountability to your rules, then you will have a much better chance of following them. I know of no other way to ensure following a rule than creating a solid agreement with someone important who has clearly delineated expectations and consequences, which also involves supervisory oversight by the person to whom the agreement was made.

I am going to tell you the ultimate secret to day trading right here and right now. Lean in close and pay attention.

As I have mentioned a number of times, in the last three years I have personally worked with over 100 traders. Every single one of them was able to use my predictable patterns to make profits. One for one. That has never been a problem. BUT . . .

EVERY
SINGLE
ONE . . .

     . . . of them, often multiple times, wiped out their profits at some point by failing to exit on a small loss per the rules, instead holding on and hoping for a recovery before selling.

And this accounts for why day traders are so often losers, even those with great strategies. The ability to coldly, emotionlessly, exit and lose money at the correct level is nearly impossible over the long-term.

Almost every one of these folks, at these moments, went through introspective self-abnegation, self-insult, talking about their lack of moral fiber, fortitude, "cowardice," and weakness. This is a sad thing, because most of these people are otherwise upstanding people by any normal measure. They are not criminals, promise-breakers, drug dealers, cheaters, or other well-known labels for people who do bad things that hurt others. These are mainly good people. To see them running themselves down like this is heartbreaking.

I've done it to myself a number of times, and I would not describe it as healthy.

I want to impart my fully qualified opinion about each of these people. Almost none of them deserve to experience the insults they level against themselves. They have been led into a trap that brings this on. The stock market makes you feel this way by making you commit these infractions and making you feel like an infraction-committer. End of story.

There is really only one solution I have found that fully prevents this, thwarting the devil in his goal to bring one to their knees.

This would involve coming up with a deal that is a concrete fail-safe for ensuring a stop loss is placed on every single trade, with someone other than you. And it has to be something that involves actual oversight. Where the person who has been promised can actually verify that you followed it *every single time* and that failing to do so results in an unmistakable penalty for noncompliance or a tangible and desirable reward for compliance. Either or both of these are vital. Counting upon yourself in the heat of the moment is near impossible over any longer period of time.

I was once trading a joint account with a close friend, with our money involved. I failed to place a stop loss, and this resulted in drawdowns on the account that were catastrophic. By the luck of the holy graces of an unseeable god or gods of our fates, it rebounded and recovered, preventing devastating losses. Oh, there were very painful losses, do not doubt that. But, then I made a solemn promise that if I ever failed to impose a stop loss on any single trade, I would be accountable to provide extensive amends of a material, clearly stated amount. Now, with this in place, in the moment when the internal urge to hold on and hope rather than to impose a stop loss becomes an all-encompassing feeling, the external threat of what happens when I break this promise of placing a stop loss is even more powerful than that internal gambler devil's influence. I place the stop loss every time now (unless the profit/loss is instantly green after the buy and I simply take a profit).

When you read this, it may appear that I am wrestling with multiple mental voices and noises, and perhaps I need professional help. . . .

That's another discussion!! And whether that is true or not, I still have not met a single trader that didn't fall for this urge as well: the urge to hold on and not sell a losing position in the hopes that it will recover. So, unless 100% of people are "schitzoid paranoids" like me, I'm most likely just human, like you. Lured into this state by the mighty market.

Therefore, I believe that having a tangible and very undesirable penalty or valuable reward for compliance (named out clearly and not generalized) with direct and clear responsibility specifically for *failing to place a stop loss*, not the general penalty for the general offense of "gambling" or "losing money" SPECIFICALLY for *no stop loss placed* on every single trade no fail, with daily oversight for every trade, is the only way to deal with the inevitable scenario of a wipe out from an unending drop of a share price while stuck in a position.

I'd like to give you an idea of how this could work.

Let us say that Bruce was a trader who wanted to succeed and understood that doing so required conquering this trap. What could he do? How could he be immunized to this disease? He goes to his neighbor, Leroy, and says, "Hey Leroy, I could use your help on something, and I will pay you $100 a month for this. And it will take you about 30 seconds of work per day."

"I'm listening," says Leroy.

"I want you to hold on to this $500 cash for me. And every day, I will send you a full screenshot of the orders I placed for my Day Trading activity. See this right here?" Bruce shows Leroy one of these screenshots, and points at the part where it names the order type, meaning if the sell order was a *Market Order,* a *Limit Order,* a *Stop Loss,* or an *OCO.*

"I am trying to keep my discipline on using stop losses to prevent big losses, but I need some accountability for this," says Bruce. He continues, "If you monitor me every day for a month, verifying that I used an OCO or a STOP LOSS for every sell order, I will let you keep $100 of that $500. But if you see one sell order that is not either a stop loss, including a trailing stop or an OCO, you keep the other $400."

"I like this game. Are there any exceptions to this?" says Leroy.

"Yes, there is one exception. If the sell is within 45 seconds of the buy, then I am off the hook for not using a stop loss," said Bruce.

"What if I don't receive a screenshot from you after trading?" asked Leroy.

"Then you have to chase me up and get me to send it," said Bruce.

Then Bruce proudly sends Leroy his screenshots every day, grandstanding his own standardness. Details of these rules are discussed and laid down on paper between the two. This type of arrangement is really the only method I know of to guarantee that Bruce will continue to use stop losses and thereby make long-term success more likely.

I've erroneously believed in the mental stop loss method as a workable thing. I know there are some successful traders out there that do it. I've never been able to maintain this over a long period, and I don't personally know anyone who has either.

What has not worked is promising someone but with no OVERSIGHT by the person promised. Or promising someone that you'll pay them later if you break your word. The friend too often gives in and feels bad and doesn't make the offender pay.

In other words, the deal has to be WATERTIGHT. And VERY SPECIFIC. If you think this whole portion sounds weird, you haven't day traded for very long.

I am starting an Accountability Club with fellow traders. I'll tell you how it will be structured. Let's say ten traders want to be part of this. On the first of the month, we all put $100 into the pot. One regulator is assigned to verify that each participant did stop losses on every trade, whether a stop on quote, OCO, or trailing stop. The only exception being if they sold within the first 45 seconds, in which case a limit order or market order is fine. Screenshots must be provided to prove this. Anyone who fails to place a stop loss on every trade is disqualified and forfeits their money. At the end, those who kept in the stop losses split the pot. This repeats monthly, or even bi-weekly, with the aim and likely result of all participants being highly profitable.

That's the final point of this lesson. Stop losses and accountability. Which is the only cure I know of for the account wipe-out that actually works for longer than a week or two.

Weird Ways

The following attitude has been a great way to prevent screwing up and losing tons. It's going to sound weird, as I promised in the title of this section. But when I veer off from these ideas and second guess them, I fail and lose. So here they are.

Number one is the attitude and belief that I am natively and inherently *unlucky*, and I possess no magic touch. And the only way to defeat this unfortunate truth is by using intelligence to outsmart my unluckiness. This hard-learned lesson comes from losing thousands upon thousands of dollars chasing down luck-driven decisions, thinking I should try out something unproven. Sadly, these unproven gambles sometimes work and then I get the idea that I am in fact "lucky." That I am "the man." That I have the "Midas touch." All of these ideas are nice to feel, and I don't think a person should be denied feeling them, but in this arena they are suicidal. Therefore, every move I make has to be backed by tested and knowledgeable facts and probabilities before I do them.

Number two, hunches, intuition, feelings, and guesses are the feed that fatten up the pig before it gets butchered. Sorry to be crass and vulgar. It's true. I stick to the pattern rules described herein or else I pay the price. Fact. Almost one for one. It's that one time that I break the rules and then it works that is the worst. It makes me formulate this new idea that my rules weren't perfectly true, that I just made a new discovery, and this discovery was innovative. Then I try it again, and I feel my internal organs get ripped out of me as I see money evaporating. Therefore, ignore hunches, intuitions, feelings, and guesses.

Number three, be stupidly happy about earning something much less than you could have. If I hear myself saying "if I just stayed in longer, I could have made more money," I usually need to remind myself that this is folly. Yesterday, I made $9,000 in 1.5 minutes. If I had stayed in, I would have made $30,000 in 4 minutes. How was I supposed to know that? I'm not Nostradamus; $9,000 in 1.5 minutes is awesome. I should be happy about it. This stock market is designed to make you feel that the next day, you hold on longer for the bigger win and get destroyed. This is another reason why only a small percentage of people make money day trading. Take those hunches, intuitions, and guesses, and flush 'em down the toilet.

In summary, when I use stop losses religiously and consider myself unlucky inherently, and create real accountability for following the rules, I succeed very well in fact. When I don't, and the allure and temptation to run off the beaten path is irresistible and I fall prey to it, I lose. It's so easy to look back and say this, so I recommend rereading this chapter after you have traded for a few weeks to keep these mindsets set in your mind.

The Stash

"I need to grow a mustache to be bulletproof?" Exactly. Just kidding. No. I mean grow one if you want, but it's a different definition of "stash."

The last part of the Bulletproof Strategy is stashing earnings. If the above steps are followed, we hope our account grows and grows. Stashing earnings away to the point where the principal investment has been completely withdrawn from the trading account ensures you are in fact bulletproof; 100% immune to losing a single dime to any market chicaneries. You would only be playing with profit, quite the ideal arrangement, of course, and completely possible.

I have not only done this myself, but I have also seen others do it. Being methodical, taking out certain amounts every week, keeping a journal, add to this systematic, technician-like approach, and while it limits your trading power by removing available investible funds, it provides more long-term success. In the summer of 2022 I did just that. I started with exactly $50,000 in my account. Every Monday before trading opened, I transferred every dollar and cent in the account that was above $50,000 into my personal bank account and started fresh. Often, this was around $2,000 to $3,000. It was a valid and substantial income source that made its way into my account rather than remaining vulnerable to loss in a trading account. Compounding one's account is not wrong. If this is your strategy, then please, go for it. One can also do both. I could have, for example, left $1,000 in the account each Monday, slowly adding to the base trading amount, giving myself more investment power. It is my opinion though, having done all three methods, pure compounding taking out nothing, removing all profits every week, or a hybrid of the two, that removing regularly was the healthiest and most successful method of all.

The Stock Market will exploit every weakness you have if you are a trader. One of those is, of course, FOMO, Fear Of Missing Out. If you combine FOMO with YOLO, you might as well kiss your money goodbye. When a strategy is applied and results in an impressive increase in account value, the trader will all-too-often start to feel both invincible and adventurous. This leads to risking even more capital, which is not a bad thing per se. But in doing so, stashing is still the only true bulletproof strategy in the end. Removing the principal from harm's way completely is the only true way to protect it.

In essence, I highly and eagerly insist that if you have a winning strategy that is making you money, keep a journal so it is very clear where things stand, and systematically withdraw money from the trading account and place it in a safe location, whether that is a slow-moving mutual fund, T-notes, a savings account, or whatever you or a financial advisor have decided is a truly safe investment or location for money. Replace the entire principal with profit and leave nothing left, and, of course, you are now 100% bulletproof, for real. This chapter is, in my opinion, the make or break of any high-risk strategy for making money.

There certainly are people out there who are doing a day trading strategy without all of this accountability puppet-string stuff tied to them and are profiting. So, I apologize if it feels like I am saying that this is an ABSOLUTE MUST. I am not. I am merely saying that it is the only way I can think of that nearly GUARANTEES the proper result.

Hope you CRUSH it, and remain bulletproof as you enter the battlefield of the stock market war games, armed with your 20-Minute Trader battle axe and shield!!

Chapter 19
Trading Update

That last chapter probably sounded a bit extreme. There is a very good reason for that. Something happened in June of 2023, last month, that explains why I have become ten times more passionate than ever before about placing stop losses and making oneself bulletproof.

By Tuesday, June 5, the account that started on May 15, 2023, had grown to $875,913.70, a 9.5% profit over only three weeks. Yeah, I was feeling pretty proud. Making over $75,000 in three weeks was certainly a new, next-level experience for me. During this three-week run, I never failed to bail at correct loss points, mostly using mental stop losses, in other words, exiting manually when down. Using this much money, and the fact that the money was partly a friend's, gave me more responsibility not to be careless or risky but to be very strict and adhere to the rules precisely.

Something weird happened on that Tuesday evening, June 6, that threw me off badly. I received an accusatory message from a friend, that she had communicated to a number of other friends, which made me look like a bad person. It bothered me mostly because it appeared that I had done dishonest things to these other friends, and it seemed plausible and seemed to have evidence to support it. It was about an investment that some people got involved in, which hadn't panned out yet, and I was part of it as well. I was a major part of it. I wasn't giving financial advice since I am not allowed to, but people did watch what I did. By pure coincidence, some of these same friends had been victimized by a scam that wiped out large amounts of money, and of course, they started wondering if the investment we got involved in was also a scam. It had a similar flavor to it, actually, which heavily concerned me.

I personally don't think that obsessively "wanting people to like you" is very honorable. If one can get over this desire, they can be a better person with high integrity. I strive to achieve this type of attitude as much as I can and, of course, I fall short on it at times. Whereas I knew these friends who received this negative message about me would think I was a two-faced piece of dog doo, my concern was maybe a tiny bit about wanting them to like me and otherwise wanting to retain their friendship and trust. I believe that friendship is the reward of living. I value it more than almost anything. I love relationships, and I love comradery. It is why I love people, most people.

It was too late on Tuesday to do anything about it, so I went to bed. I could barely sleep that night, and I woke at 3:30 a.m. Wednesday worried, trying to formulate a solution in my head. I finally got up and started to write an email to everyone involved, disproving the allegations, trying not to be defensive, and trying not to rundown the friend who sent the message. It was hard to do. I was emotional. I ping-ponged between feeling angry at her and understanding her. After a couple of hours of this, I was drained. I had rewritten this two-page email ten or so times, and I felt not only exhausted from the low sleep and the adrenaline, but also still just as worried as when I first saw the message the night before. It was in this wired, ragged state that I entered the market on Wednesday morning, June 7.

My first trade was at 9:33 and 21 seconds. I sold at 9:34 and 21 seconds, exactly one minute later, with a profit of $2,500, bringing the account to almost $880,000. But I was not satisfied with this amount, and I wanted more. So, I placed another trade at 9:35 and 15 seconds. This one did not result in a rally of the stock, but instead dropped down and erased the $2,500 profit I had just enjoyed. I quickly scanned the buy point I had chosen and noted that it was actually missing one or two of the criteria I use to determine a good signal. I should've simply bailed at that point and cut my losses. Instead, I held on and sought a retrieval of the lost profits. The stock took a nose dive so far that I was tens of thousands of dollars in the red. Many tens. By the time I had completed the trade I had lost $67,000 of the account, which now stood with a value of around $810,000. My profit of nearly $80,000 was wiped out down to only $10,000.

The truth of the matter is it was even lower than that at some points. And I kept holding until it came back up to "only" a $67,000 loss. But that was pure luck, pure gamble. The next few trading days were not much better. I was on tilt, and I tried to make back the losses rather than just accepting small profits. In doing so, I held on when I should have sold in the green, and dropped the account all the way down to $756,228.85, about $44,000 in the red from our principal.

One of my friends called me who knew exactly what I was going through, especially since I published all of my trades readily and with transparency.

"Hey Jeremy, I want to tell you something I heard a guy say one time that I think applies to you here," he said.

"Yeah?" I answered.

"Stop trying to make it all back in one trade," he said.

He was dead on. Totally correct. I went back to what I was doing before, and I aimed for a little bit of daily green. I also kept my stop losses in hard. I made a deal with my co-investor that this would always remain the case, and I included oversight and exacting penalties and rewards for my compliance. Now, today, at the end of July, with an average gain per day of only $5,700, the account value is $940,952.25. And this included several days of getting stopped out with stop losses.

This is why I became so passionate about stop losses and accountability. Because it worked for me, massively. There is also that little gem about not trying to make it all back in one trade.

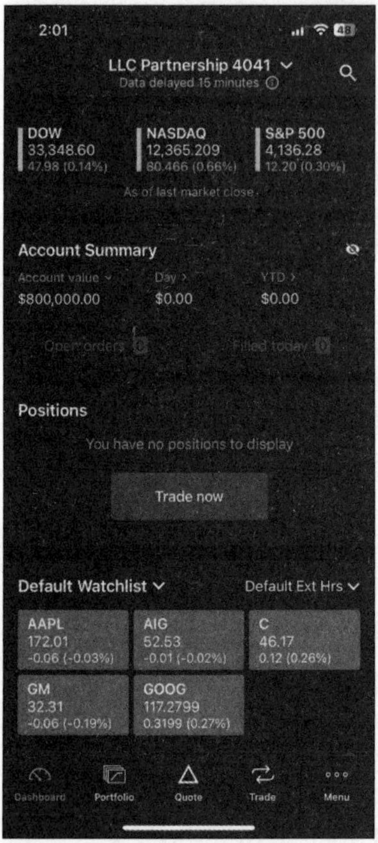

FIGURE 19.1
May 15

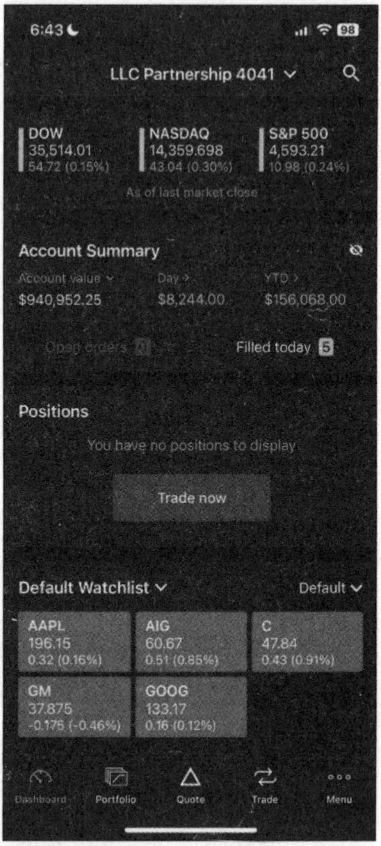

FIGURE 19.2
July 31

Chapter 20
Now What Should I Do?

I know I have machine-gunned a bunch of info. Now, it is time to summarize and give you the exact play-by-play instructions on what to do next.

"Why didn't I just skip to this part? I had to sit through all that to get here?"

I'm sure you will do better as a result. It's one thing to know the steps of something. It's quite another to understand them. Now you do, or hopefully you do. So, as I lay these out, you should have a better grasp of what to do based on a deeper understanding.

I will lay this out step-by-step as if you have done nothing and have never traded before. As you do each of these steps, refer to the chapter that gives more details about each.

Step 1.

Sign up for a trading account.

As you sign up for this account, ensure the following:

Sign up for a cash (not a margin) account.
   Sign up for Level II options trading.
   Sign up for a paper trading account.

If any of the above conditions are not met, you may not be able to employ this system. One little tip: if while signing up for this account, you are asked what the intention is, and you say, "income," they will likely refuse to grant you the account. There is another choice that contains the word "speculation." This is the one that I did.

For all questions asked and boxes to check, be honest, and if the question is confusing, do your best!

Step 2.

Sign up for the Premium membership on TradingView using this link for the maximum savings for you:

`https://www.tradingview.com/?aff_id=26705`

It must be the Premium membership or you will not get the one-second charts. I am sorry that this is the most expensive one offered. I wish it weren't, but it's the one we need.

Step 3.

Set up the charts. (If you want the one-click chart setup or need help navigating this at any point, simply go to my website, click the chat box, and someone should be able to assist you right away.)

Otherwise, you may go back to Chapter 10 and follow the exact steps listed there.

Step 4.

Choose a ticker.

Think of a big company that you like. I'd avoid any evil companies that truly hurt people and make money in the process. I kind of believe in karma, which could include some drug or pesticide companies.

Use your search engine to find the Ticker symbol.

Plug the Ticker symbol onto your TradingView charts by clicking the existing ticker and then typing in the one you want.

Bring your cursor to the bottom of the chart and click on the 5y button.

If the stock shows good, steady growth over those years, it should be fine.

Step 5.

Return to the one-second time frame. Go to the beginning of the market (9:30 EST). Scan the next 20-minute time period for a U-shape that should repeat several times. These are usually about one to a few minutes long from drop to rise.

Make careful notes of the motions of the Dow Jones just before the rise (during the bottom part of the U), such as a divergent motion that seemed to have inspired the stock's follow-up rise. Make exacting notes of this. As you look over each of the U-shapes, make the same notations.

Repeat this action daily until you have determined what the Dow motion is that seems to predict this jump in your stock.

If there seems to be no correlation between the Dow's motions and the stock's after-motions, select another index (such as the S&P 500 or the NASDAQ). And repeat the above steps. If there is still no relationship, choose another ticker.

Do this for up to four weeks until you have enough information to form a conclusion about what the predictor is. I highly suggest not using an "expert" or "extra set of eyes" to assist on this; use your own observations and conclusions. Write down detailed specifics on durations and magnitudes.

Write down the rules. These could be something like, "The Dow Jones sometimes jumps 20 points just before the stock rally, after the two lines sync for 15 seconds, and this seems to be the predictor."

Step 6.

Practice paper trading the pattern rules you have adopted. This means you are using fake money rather than real money but in the real market. It allows you to try out a strategy without having to lose any real money doing so.

When you sign into your account, ensure you are on the paper trading setting rather than the real trading setting.

Go to the trade page and select Calls.

Choose an expiry that is not today but not two weeks from today, right in between.

Select a strike price that causes your Contract price to be in the range that you desire.

Change the buy order type from Limit to Market.

Watch for the buy signal.

When you see the buy signal, "purchase" the call option.

Go to your positions and note that you have this security in your portfolio.

Watch the charts for the stock's share price value line to go up.

When it does, sell off the position for a profit by tapping the position, hitting "close," changing the order type to *market*, and then hitting *preview*, then *send*.

If it goes down, wait to see how far, and take note. It may go right back up. If it does not and continues to drop, sell off the position and make a note of how much you lost.

Make a note of how far the stock dropped for you to have lost this amount.

After paper trading a few dozen times and noting the profits and losses, choose your exit strategy precisely. This means that at a certain drop value, one should exit. This exit point should remain a hard rule for future trading.

Test out these rules over the next week, doing one to four trades per 20-minute time period.

If profitable, you've got your system!!! If not, you may need to adjust your take-profit target or your exit levels to adjust for mitigating losses or capturing more gains.

For example, you may notice that the stock always rises higher than where you took profit and that waiting a little longer for more profit is a better system. Or you may note that you are exiting at a loss too fast, not allowing the stock price some breathing room to fall a little before a rally.

These analytics are vital for finalizing your strategy.

Once finalized, STICK TO IT!!

Step 7.

Write out your plan for stashing cash when profiting. How much will you take and when, in order to recoup the principal?

In conclusion

These are the simple step-by-step ways of using a predictable pattern to hopefully profit in the market!

Chapter 21
Is 20-Minute Trading Really That Easy?

I'm going to share a more in-depth version of the story of discovery, so that you can see what pitfalls I fell into, what opportunities presented themselves, and what huge mistakes or good choices I made along the way.

Why would I share this?

Because I think people think I got lucky on this, and I make it look easy. But it was not easy, and I am actually inherently unlucky. I was able to outsmart my bad luck while making devastating mistakes along the way—mistakes I do not want you to make.

I used to work at a non-profit where people could go to volunteer and learn to help others, whether with literacy, relationships, drug abuse, or any other existing life factors.

I had the chance to meet and really get to know people from many walks of life. Poor people, gang members, druggies, rich people, foreigners, homeless, educators, entrepreneurs, lawyers, doctors, actors (famous and not famous), directors, writers, artists, office workers, managers, blue collar, white collar, clean collar, dirty collar, backward collar. I met suicidal people, depressed people, panicky people, happy people, disabled people, calm people, super-abled people, professional athletes, gay, straight, lesbian, racist, anti-racist, criminal, homophobic, activists, anti-homophobic, philanthropic, greedy, generous, fat, skinny, tall, short, dying, young, old, every ethnicity you can think of, many cultures and religions, Sikhs, Jews, Muslims, Nation of Islam, Christians, Hindu, and the list can go on and on.

I met several thousand people and had many conversations with each. Not just a meet and greet. Real friendship in many cases. Being completely against some things, like racism, for instance, I didn't necessarily befriend every person I met, but I did attempt to understand. Fascinatingly, if you are interested in someone, genuinely, they will tell you almost anything and everything and usually quite excitedly.

How would you feel if someone was deeply interested in your life, and wanted to know all about it? People react quite openly in my experience, and they tell you, it seems, almost everything.

Well, I am deeply interested in others and I also care a lot about people doing well and succeeding. So, as I learned about Joe's life and found what he did that was successful or unsuccessful, I'd try to help Bob with what I learned, if the same scenarios that Joe encountered presented themselves in Bob's life. I could tell Bob what Joe went through and hopefully add to his bucket of knowledge to draw conclusions and decisions from. This has been an ongoing hobby my whole life. As a result, I have even introduced couples who have been married for years (about eight couples), helped people boom their businesses, saved their relationships, repaired things with their kids, and had all sorts of fun happenings. I've also messed up in my attempts to help others and gave crappy advice, told people the wrong story that didn't help at all, or in some cases made things worse.

As I said earlier, I had a negative opinion about the field of day trading. It didn't seem like honest work that provided a service to the world and seemed no different than gambling. So, on pure moral principle, I was against it. I even warned my family members, telling them about the nine day traders I knew, all of whom except one were unhealthy spiritually and physically in my estimation.

At 42, having just given 22 years of my possible wealth-building time to basically volunteer to help others for very little pay, I was in a hurry to catch up. That doesn't mean I was okay with giving up my scruples. But my wife was 34, and the clock was ticking.

"It's now or never on a family," she said. "But I don't want to be struggling and trying to raise kids at the same time."

I had moved into my brother's spare room in an apartment in Pasadena, California. He had just made some great money on Tesla shares and was taking a little vacation from work, enjoying his financial freedom for a bit.

It was fun bonding with him after living separately for a couple decades. We talked a lot about the world and what kinds of things I could do. I was considering taking up acting again.

I was nine years old in 1987 and was "discovered" by the mother of a pretty famous actor, who told my mother that I'd crush it in that business. This mother called the agency representing her son and asked them to meet with me and discuss taking me on. I remember going into an office and sitting down in a waiting area. Then, I was called into a room. A lady handed me a piece of paper and asked me to read it aloud and act it out.

I forgot to mention that I was so unbelievably undersized that I looked 5 years old. I was 42 inches and 40 pounds. But my reading level was at about that of an 11-year-old. So, I honestly looked like that baby from the movie *Who Framed Roger Rabbit?* That movie was making fun of the movie industry, and one thing the movie industry is notorious for is hiring older kids to play younger kids for the obvious reasons that they are usually better at taking and following directions and are also legally allowed to work longer hours. Some of us GenX-ers or older recall the show *Webster*, in which a Emmanuel Lewis was the star. Only he wasn't a little kid, he was in his teens but had a defective gene situation causing him have a shorter stature.

Here I was, a 9-year-old, with an 11-year-old reading level, who looked 5. After I read the paper for them, they signed me up in eight seconds. This was no generic agency either. These guys represented some big-time kid actors at the time. I think they represented Kirk Cameron and Fred Savage, who were two of the top kid actors back then.

Two days after I started with this agency, I was sent on an audition. My mother took me to an office in Hollywood. We walked in, filled out my name on a clipboard, and sat down. Sitting in the waiting area were a bunch of unruly kids and their moms. I say "unruly" because I was the oldest kid there. The part was for a six-year-old, and most of the kids there were six and more unruly than us nine-year-olds.

They called in four of us at once, and we lined up in front of a mat. It turns out, they expected us to be expert gymnasts. The four kids in front of me proceeded to take turns stating their names and ages, and then performing crazy flips and handsprings across the mat. I couldn't believe six-year-olds could do this stuff. By the time it was my turn, I told them I could do a cartwheel and that's about it. I did the cartwheel, they loved me, and called me back. It came down to me and another kid, and the other kid got the part because they needed a blondie to match the parents they chose. This was for Crispix cereal.

I didn't care that I didn't get the part, especially because within the next 25 auditions I did, I booked five major, lucrative commercials and started building a decent resume. Over the next few years, I did 15 to 20 commercials, a couple TV episodes, some music videos, and a TV movie with Paul Rudd in it (I think he was 16 when we filmed it—he was really cool, by the way).

After my first commercial booking, I became a member of the Screen Actors Guild and retained the membership for the rest of my adult life, until now. When I was 14, I quit acting because I was shy and unhappy with people coming up to me and asking me if I was "the Apple Jacks guy."

Technically, I was the Apple Jacks guy, but I didn't think of myself as the Apple Jacks guy. I thought of myself as just a guy who didn't want any extra attention. I still looked about ten, but my voice had changed and was deep. Ten-year-old with a deep voice. Awkward.

When I was with my brother in his Pasadena apartment in 2019, I told him I thought about trying my hand at acting again. I called my old agent from back in the 1990s and asked him if I could come visit. He remembered me and, in fact, remembered everything about me. He knew the names of my family members and asked about them. Not having seen him in 30 years, it was fun catching up. While he was rather encouraging, he presented the odds of success in the field and they were rather discouraging. It was so easy when I was a kid. I made a boatload of cash back then. But the landscape was different, and what it takes to make it had become pretty crazy. I asked him if he would represent me, and he said he was retiring and wouldn't be able to, but otherwise would have loved to.

"Nowadays, you need to have reels of your work to present to casting directors. Scenes showing different skills that you have, and it's best if these are from real productions rather than things you would have made up yourself. Although that is better than nothing," he said.

I didn't feel like this would be a winner for me. I returned to my brother's place and thought about other ways to make a good viable living. I had decent skills as a carpenter, so I took a couple of jobs building fences and gates for upscale houses. They paid well and were fun, and I considered doing this. I put it on my list.

As I said earlier, being a semi-skilled artist (pencil drawing), I landed a few commissions to draw things. This was also fun, and I added it to my list of venture possibilities. I also started writing the book on public speaking that I talked about earlier in the book because when I was working at the non-profit, I ended up with this random job of coaching novices into being able to do speeches. I had discovered a sure-fire way to kill stage fright in the process. I also gained some local distinction for my speech-giving skills, which were incredibly bad at first but improved over time.

While all of this was happening, I was still eating and paying for gas using the little bits of credit I had left on my cards, carefully ignoring the degree of severity of my mounting debt.

My brother was trading options in the stock market every morning.

"You know, I don't really think that activity is worthwhile for this world," I told him.

"I like it," he said.

We philosophized about the rights and wrongs of trading. While doing so, I remembered Tina, a friend of mine who was an office worker at a landscaping company in Los Angeles. She once told me that she was $60,000 in debt. She was holding her young son, Trevor, who was about three years old.

"Do you have a partner that helps on the bills?" I asked.

"No. I am a single mother."

She was kind of a slave to the system. She needed her 9-to-5 job or would live in hell.

I met about a thousand Tinas during those decades—good people making too little. I also met some traders making way more money than Tina.

It became clear to me that wages are just low enough to keep you in debt, so you can pay interest on credit cards, and make ends meet barely but never really get ahead enough to have freedom over your time. And yet it is the work of good people that keeps the shops open, the companies going, the schools and services running, that we all enjoy, and which make our lives better. It seems unfair that those who keep the world turning cannot enjoy the fruits that money can bring. Meanwhile, these traders who give nothing to this world can be paid as if they are valuable to others, most of whom are not. Technically, if you balanced the books, Tina owned almost nothing.

As I remembered all this, sitting with Kris in Pasadena, it seemed like any career path I chose would wind me up in debt and indentured. He said he'd show me how options work. I looked over his shoulder as he sat on his brown leather couch and scanned through piles of symbols and numbers on his laptop. None of it made any sense to me.

Sitting next to me, he asked, "What stock do you think is going to go up today?"

"Umm...Tesla," I answered, one of the few stocks I had heard of.

"Okay. Let's buy some Tesla call options and see what happens," he said.

He paid $300 for some Tesla calls. By the end of the day they were worth $600, and he sold them. The stock had rocketed up by several dollars that morning. I was pretty fascinated. He started to tell me about earnings calls for tech companies and other little features of the market.

"What are earnings calls?" I asked.

"Announcements from public companies about how much money they made during a quarter of the year. Share prices of companies tend to spasm at earnings calls. People have an expectation for that company's earnings. If they come in higher than expectations, the share price tends to rocket. If they come in lower than the expectation, the share price tends to fall," my brother said.

The funny part is, it's not so much whether the actual amount of money earned by the company is rising or falling in comparison to its previous levels, it's more about beating or failing to beat expectations. I didn't know or understand this until later.

A few days after that Tesla call thing with Kris, I found out that the food company Beyond Meat was about to issue its earnings call. I thought that if its earnings call showed an increase in productivity compared to last quarter, this would then cause the share price to fly up. I recalled that Beyond Meat struck deals with restaurants and grocery stores to offer their products in massive volumes. I was sure the earnings call would show an incredible increase. I decided this was an easy bet! So, I took $1,000 out of my bank account, which was a large chunk of my total net worth, and I bought a call option for the Beyond Meat company a day before its earnings call.

I thought I was clever. I sat on a stool in Kris's living room, thinking of how easy it is to make money doing this stuff. I watched the financial news as they announced that Beyond Meat had brought in something like ten times the revenue this quarter compared to last. Insane expansion! I was so excited. I watched the Beyond Meat share price on a chart start twitching. It looked like the little wiggle of a child waiting for his mother to open the door of the toy store. It was about to launch up and print money for me!!

Like a lead ball dropped into a pool, the stock price fell. I saw the value of my call option contract go from $1,000 to $800 to $600 to $400 in the span of four minutes.

A month earlier, I visited the home of a wealthy couple with two lovely dogs on their property that needed to be kept in the backyard so that when cars came in and out of the driveway, they would be safe and wouldn't run out into the street.

They hired me to build a gate that matched their house's style. It had to be very strong while simple and aesthetic. I used redwood to match their wrap-around decking. Rather than using bolts and screws, I used mortise and tenon joints to construct the whole gate, hand-crafting each element with a chisel. It was 12 hours of work for one gate before I mounted it on hinges.

That part of the project paid me $800.

As I watched the $800 I earned from that skilled labor evaporate right before my eyes, I thought of the meticulous care I put into this woodworking project, the joyous feeling I had when the individually carved pieces all fit together to form a solid, beautiful gate, the expressions of happiness that my customers displayed when they saw the final result, and the pride I felt when they handed me the check.

In four minutes, all of that prideful hard work was worthless; 12 hours of work gone in a flash.

"Why did the share price drop when the earnings were so fricking high?" I asked my brother in a shaking voice of shock, and dewy eyes.

"I don't really know. I have a friend who is an expert at this stuff. I'll call him."

Thirty seconds later I hear the voice of a guy named Frank through the speaker phone.

"Hello?" said Frank.

"Hey, how come Beyond Meat's share price crashed after beating their highest ever earnings by ten X?" Kris asked.

"Cuz Wall Street expected them to do 20X. TenX was way down from there."

I jumped in.

"Wait . . . so even though the company expanded in size by tenfold in one quarter, analysts expected them to do so by 20 times, and were disgusted with this tenX result?" I asked.

"Basically," he said.

This was a new concept to me. In my world, a person's production gives them relative value. If Sharon could sell more widgets than Brian, she was paid more than Brian. What I heard from Frank is that Wall Street is another layer. If they bet that Brian was going to sell five widgets, and Sharon was going to sell ten, but Brian sold six, and Sharon sold nine, Brian's value would jump and Sharon's would drop, even though Sharon was outselling Brian, simply because of estimates.

Turns out that estimates are INCREDIBLY important figures on Wall Street.

Learning this lesson while bleeding out from the Beyond Meats injury, I decided to hold on to the contract and see if perhaps the share price went back up and recovered maybe a little. The contract still had two days until expiry. The share price drifted up and down, but mostly down over the next two days.

The value of my $1,000 contract was now down to $5. Finally, on that Friday at 12:59 p.m., there was one minute left until the contract expired. The strike price I had chosen was now much higher than the existing share price of the stock. The likelihood of the share price jumping up and meeting this strike price in the last minute by several dollars was close to zero.

My brother was sitting on his couch, and I was standing by the kitchen counter.

"The option is about to expire and is only worth five bucks now," I said.

"How much time left?" asked Kris.

"Twenty-five seconds until the market closes. Should I at least try to sell it and make back five bucks? Who the hell would buy it?" I asked.

"Yeah, give it a try!" said Kris.

I placed a sell order for $5 for this contract. Two seconds before the 1 p.m. closing bell, someone bought the contract from me for $5.

"Someone bought it!" I said.

"What?" said Kris.

"What the hell was this guy thinking?" I asked.

In a high-pitched nerdy guy voice, imitating whoever it was that bought this from me, Kris said, "I think the share price is going to jump up in the next few seconds!! Here's five dollars!!"

Over the next several minutes Kris and I laughed so hard, with multiple imitations of this guy who just gave me five bucks for no reason whatsoever, and no value in return, with a couple seconds left until expiry. Our stomachs hurt.

It was a welcomed glee from the burn of the loss.

After we recovered from our mirth, I realized bluntly that the main and most obvious fact about the stock market is that it is UNPREDICTABLE.

I called Frank, "Hey man, how do we know where a stock is going to go?"

"That's basically impossible to know. There are things that are more likely than others, but no assurances at any point or any time on anything," he said.

The stock market had unsympathetically robbed me of my hard-earned money. I felt mugged, abused, taken advantage of.

I couldn't forgive Wall Street for mugging me. I ended up watching charts.

If the consensus of Wall Street was that it was simply never going to be predictable, I didn't even want to know what these people knew. I didn't want to hear about any strategy, system, or anything that someone purported to know, because I was now in a place where the idea was failure. Not unlike the viewpoint of my former acting agent about the potential of success in acting these days.

"Failure is the main result," is the slogan I kept hearing about trading.

I was afraid to hear what other people were doing because it was all on the premise that it was impossible.

It reminded me of the time in high school when I succeeded at basketball, despite my smaller stature. Point being, when I hear that something is impossible, I am often inspired to crack the code.

By this point it was November 2019, and as I said, I watched stock charts trying to figure out how to know where it would go without asking anyone. After a month, I started to realize that every morning, in the first ten or so minutes of the market, this one stock just dropped and rose in the shape of a U—every single day.

I was trying to figure out how to guess when it planned to jump back up after its drop, the first half of the U.

As I said earlier, Kris said he thought this stock and the Dow Jones had some sort of a relationship. I decided to try watching the Dow Jones chart over the chart of this tech stock with the U shape. I noticed that often when the two lines (one of the tech stock and one of the Dow values) dropped in sync, and then the Dow broke away upward, the tech Stock then began its ascent to complete the second half of the U. During this, I was talking a lot to Frank and Kris trying to understand what options really were. We watched multiple YouTube videos that honestly made ZERO sense to me. These videos would give the correct definition, but I felt the definitions were too detailed rather than what these things were to traders. It would be like asking for the definition of "water" and being told that hydrogen was the smallest element in the periodic table, oxygen was a gas, and the bond between these creates molecules that aggregate into a liquid that has conductive properties. All true but completely useless. A better definition for the layperson would be to say that water is the clear liquid that all mammals need to consume to survive and quench thirst, and it's what rain, oceans, rivers, lakes, and ponds are made of—something like that.

Frank was a swing trader. He held these options contracts for weeks, so this was the closest thing to a strategy that I knew of. I tried this out with a $100 here and there, while I continued to pursue other career avenues. I continued writing my public speaking book, doing carpentry jobs, and drawing pictures. But I also got an idea that I thought could really build wealth!

I felt like I could take a group or activity and make it expand and succeed through sheer intention. I could find a way to exploit opportunities, push things to a more efficient production system, accelerate marketing and sales, and build systems to make all this happen. The only reason I thought I could do this was because it is what I did in any department I was part of in the non-profit I worked for. It was something I liked doing and felt I had a talent for.

So, I thought about my friend, Stephanie.

I had not seen her for years but recalled chatting with her in 2014 about her Etsy custom throw pillow business. It was around November of that year, and she complained that her sales were barely good enough to keep the operation going, and she really needed to make more money. I asked her about 20 questions regarding the business, and then I gave her a suggestion. Looking at her listings, she had about four sample custom throw pillows with cute phrases or pictures on them. These were great gifts, and she was making $4,000 per month doing this.

"How do you get photos of these pillows?" I asked.

"It's a lot of work. I have to create the pillow, set up the lighting, stage them, and then photograph them."

"I see. Want to make $20,000 in December?"

"Heck yeah!" she said.

"Go on Fivvr, find a photoshop expert, and come up with 50 designs or phrases that people might like. Get the photoshop person to take these nice photos you have and change out the message on the pillows."

"Hmmm. Interesting," she said.

"Choose your favorite 30 and put 'em up for sale. Think holiday gifts," I said.

She did it. On December 12, she had to shut her site down to spend the next two weeks fulfilling her $26,000 worth of orders. She couldn't handle any more if they came in.

We both carried on with our lives, but I never forgot how much I thought to myself that I could really go in there and figure out how to boom her business.

December 12, 2019, I looked at my bank account and my credit balances. The bank was a few thousand and the credit balances were several tens of thousands. I was still technically homeless since I was living with my brother impermanently. My wife was still in another city wrapping up her job. I remember thinking that December 12 was the same day that Stephanie had to shut down her listings to have time to fulfill orders during the holidays.

I thought of her and envisioned my idea to make her and me money. But I knew she wouldn't be available until the new year with all the holiday traffic she would be dealing with. So, I held off calling her. Every day, my credit card balances grew, and my bank account shrank.

The holidays came, and I spent even more money, going out to visit my 90-year-old grandmother, who I would honestly have spent my last penny going to see; I love her so much, but I was running on fumes.

I had tried about 15 swing trades, most of which were flops. I was starting to see fast-food work or Uber driving in my future if I didn't come up with something. Neither of these professions would bring the lifestyle my wife and I wanted to build a family.

I finally called Stephanie and asked her to meet up. She agreed, and I drove to Santa Monica to have coffee with her. It was such a lovely January day, 68 degrees, breezy. It's a day that elucidates why LA weather is so nice. The salty wind from the Pacific made its way into my nostrils and then into the memory of this moment.

"Hi Steph!"

"Hey Jer!!"

We sat and sipped on coffee, wearing shades on that bright afternoon.

"I have a business idea I want to propose," I said.

"Oh interesting! I had no idea what this meeting was going to be about, but I am intrigued," she said.

"It's about your pillow thing. I think I can double your revenue. And if so, I wanted to share the new profits."

"I really don't want to do more work," she said. Stephanie was almost 50 and was a decently successful actress. She was so incredibly young looking for her age; it was magic. She had recently played the girlfriend of a 25-year-old man, who looked about 30, and her character was supposed to be the same age. Remarkable, really. In Hollywood though, you can be a working actor and still be broke. The gap between making a killing and being poor in Hollywood is not unlike the gap between successful options day traders and those that lose money. We're talking low single-digit percentages for those that can survive on the earnings.

At Stephanie's age, her level of hustle in her Etsy business, and her acting career, taking on more work was really the last thing she wanted to do with her time.

"Don't worry, you'll have little or nothing more to do than you already do. I will do everything from my end to add value to your production line and sales."

"Seems like a win-win if that's true," she said.

We agreed on a deal. I, of course, knew less than zero about Etsy, making pillows, or getting people to buy pillows, but I knew the potential was there and wasn't fully exploited.

"I need food and gas money and I am too proud to ask anyone but Chase, BofA, or Capital One," I said to Kris.

"Well, you can stay here as long as you need to save on rent," said Kris.

"I can't thank you enough," I replied.

"Thanks for keeping the place clean all the time!" he said.

"It's the least I can do."

I started digging in on this pillow business idea with Stephanie, frequently going to her workshop, checking out her operations, and looking for ways to make things more productive and augment sales. She had added some products to her Etsy store, including a gift box with soap and a little succulent plant. I found myself driving around the city helping her source these things, which cost me gas money, but was part of the investment.

One day in early 2020, before the pandemic hit, driving back from Orange County with a few trays of succulents in the back of my car, I pulled over to a gas station to fuel up. I looked over my credit and debit cards to choose which one to use. Most of them were running low on available credit, and the debit card was showing a lower balance than I thought. I used one of the cards to fill up the tank and the total was about $100.

"I need to get at least some flow of money in. This is getting unsustainable," I thought.

I delivered the plants to Stephanie and went home. I logged in to my Capital One credit card online banking portal and requested a high percent cash advance.

Then, I transferred some money into my brokerage account and decided that I was going to try to play the U-shape I had seen so many times on the tech stock I was watching at the end of 2019 and in early 2020.

"I just need to make a few bucks for food and gas, and this is the only thing in the stock market that I can predict," I thought.

The next morning, I woke up at my usual early hour, went over to my laptop, and opened up a chart. The market opened, I waited for the pattern to present itself, and nervously bought a call option for $1,080. The following minutes felt like a lifetime . . . but the jump happened exactly as I predicted and . . . I sold for $1,130 exactly. I made my first $50 using the predictable pattern. This was great; I had a way to make food and gas money before going to work every day.

So, the next day, I did the same thing. And I made $199.

Then, on my next trade I made $300. The next day, I made $185.

As I continued to work on the pillow thing, I kept using this hack to make extra dough.

I asked my friend Sean for help on the Etsy thing. We came up with an idea to make a parallel Shopify store so we could have as much marketing as we wanted since the Etsy store had limitations.

Sean and I were as green as the slime on the 1990s Nickelodeon kid shows. But we also felt that learning this was a genius idea to get a platform for any sales venture we may partake in.

We set up the store, placed the pillows on display, and started advertising them. Sales came trickling in, which was really fun, to be honest.

We filmed ads, promoted the product, and otherwise did the best we could to drive sales. Meanwhile, I told Sean about my trading strategy. He was immediately interested and asked me to teach him. Over the phone, I described the method. He tried it out and loved it. It was making him money almost every day. So, I taught my other friend Camilla, then Cody, then Ray, then Juan, then a couple of others.

My friend Todd asked me over for dinner at his apartment in LA. Todd made sous vide filet mignon, which was awesome. I described my trading method, and he said he wanted to learn it. I was happy to teach him.

"How much will you charge to teach me?" he asked.

"Huh?" I said.

"Name your price," he responded.

"I wasn't planning to charge you anything!" I said.

"You should. It's an amazing service," he argued.

"I'm not even sure its legal to charge someone for this since I am not a registered financial advisor," I argued.

"Well, make it legal and sell it to me," he said.

I found out that if you publish a generic strategy for trading or investment, without giving individualized custom advice, then you're covered under the Publisher's Exemption. So, I set it up that way and he paid me to teach him, which I did, and which he loved. He started making not unimpressive money.

Meanwhile, the pillow store was rolling. I wasn't making a killing, but Sean and I were learning, and we were profitable. Shopify sent us a notification that we were in the top ten percent of earnings for new Shopify stores.

By this point, my wife and I had moved into a 700-square-foot apartment in Brentwood so that she could be close to her work in Westwood. She had started working for a law firm as an assistant, and was covering more of the bills than I was, giving me some breathing room to try my startups. But we were still living paycheck to paycheck.

After I got my first payment from Todd, I went online and signed up for an LLC of my own.

On the pillow sales, our big plan was to capitalize on Mother's Day, the perfect way to sell these customized pillows. One particular pillow had sold quite well on Etsy, which showed a map of the United States with a few hearts placed on a few cities, with a caption, "Love Lives Here." I got one for my mother in May 2020, and she liked it.

To try to sell this product, I made two video ads. I was in one of them, and my wife was in the other. I talked about the custom pillows, how they are made on demand, and how nice they are. I also filmed my wife saying the same stuff. Sean wanted to run both ads and see which one performed better.

When we ran these ads on Facebook, it was super clear that my wife's ad was about one thousand times more successful than the one I did. Since you can comment on Facebook ads, I looked over what folks were saying about hers and about mine. Hers were full of good questions and "Thank yous," while mine were mostly propositions from gay men asking if I was available or telling me I was cute. HA-HA, I learned something about branding, audiences, and advertising that day!

After the Mother's Day sale was done, we regrouped and checked the numbers. I had made a personal profit of $2,500 over the span of three months doing this store with Sean and Stephanie. Now, it was time to present my future business plan to Stephanie.

I stood in my living room and called her.

"The store was a small success, but we now have the elements to take this to the next level," I said. I went on to describe how we could scale up, and make her rich within two years, while making myself a decent living along the way.

"You know, I make more than enough working about three or four hours a day already. Working with you these last few months, I had to work a bit more. And I just really don't need it, and that extra work . . . I just don't want to do it," she said.

I felt my stomach hit the floor, and then my heart replaced my stomach's former location. Three months of learning, building, selling, optimizing, and finally profiting, I saw a bright future. The product Stephanie made was loved by all and quite scalable. I was envisioning this as fantastic way to gain control of my life and my pay for the work I was doing. But she was clear. The answer was no.

Respectfully, I accepted her refusal. I probably could have talked her into letting me keep going, but I knew she would not be into it. And that alone would kill the vibe for the group.

I am not complaining about Stephanie here and am not the least bit critical of her choice. Even at the time, I wasn't mad at her in the least, nor did I feel she was being unfair in any way. In fact, I was truly grateful that she let me into her world and allowed me to learn it, be part of it, and even contribute to it. We simply had unmatched ambitions.

The result, though, is that I was again the new kid in school, coming in mid-semester, knowing no one and having no footing. I was back at square zero, and no closer to having the life setup we needed to begin a family.

"Hey Jess, what would we have to do in order for you to feel good about having a kid?" I asked my wife.

"I want to be more financially secure before we take on that adventure," she replied.

"What would that mean for you? Like literally?" I asked.

"What do you mean?" she asked.

"I mean, like how much money would we have to have for you to feel safe enough to bring a kid into this world?"

"We would need to have ten months of our expenses covered so that in the event we have no money coming in we can still afford to live," she said.

"Okay, so once we have that in the bank, you're ready?"

"Yeah."

I now had an exact metric to aim for, so that my dream of becoming a father could come true.

We had discussed many times how so many families start without having the financial stability that she described. Most do not have this and yet the family gets going and the children end up okay. But that wasn't what she wanted. She was scared. What if the pregnancy is so bad that she can't work during it? What if after the baby is born, she is unable to work and provide? At that time, she was the primary breadwinner, and I was the wildcard. Who knew if this would ever work? While she believed in me, she was also a realist.

So, the game was afoot. I had to make this money and fill up the till so that I could get going on the adventure I cared about more than anything—the adventure of parenthood.

Trading was going better and better as the summer of 2020 rolled out. Covid lockdowns made the stay-at-home retail traders get busy. Trading hobbyists opened brokerage accounts like they were going out of style, and trading gurus started cashing in.

I was getting calls off the hook to learn my method, and I found myself spending all day teaching people while spending only 20 minutes in the morning doing the trades and making nice cash.

The goal was becoming more realistic as the credit card debt pile was getting smaller, and the bank account and brokerage accounts were getting bigger.

My wife, Jessica, had been hanging out with our friend Cristina, and found out that Cristina's husband, Kevin, was a videographer by trade specializing specifically in making video courses. Both of them were long-time friends but we hadn't seen them in years. Jessica brought up the idea to Cristina to have Kevin make me a video course to help deal with the inflow of requests to learn my system, which by this point I had named "20-Minute Trader."

I met with Kevin, and he loved the idea. We set a date, I wrote out a script, and we filmed the whole thing over two days.

When people called to learn about 20-Minute Trading, I was able to give them my video course, enabling me to take on more people.

Keep in mind I wasn't even trying to start a business with this. I was just sitting there doing my trading and helping people learn my method.

I was also commissioned to draw a portrait for someone. So, I had three sources of income: teaching the strategy, trading, and drawings.

My bank account was filling up as I withdrew winnings from my brokerage. By October, I needed $15,500 more to hit the goal we had set for being ready financially to start a family. Right then, I took out that exact amount from my brokerage account.

By that point, I had been able to withdraw $27,000 from my trading account and finally put in the last penny I needed to fulfill Jessica's request about feeling ready to embark on having children.

"Hey Jess, let me show you something."

"What?"

I showed her the account balance in my bank account. It was the exact number that we had agreed upon, ten months of expenses covered.

In December, we got the positive pregnancy test.

By this time, I was sending out my video to anyone who asked and paid for it, never promoting it or even making it known through any means. It was 100% word of mouth. But something crazy happened with my trading that threw everything for a loop.

A well-off friend of mine begged me to trade for him. I said no repeatedly. I wasn't ready, and didn't even think it was legal. Turns out you can have a joint account with someone, and either of you can access and trade it. He repeatedly assured me that I could lose the full principal and he would be completely fine with it.

We funded it with $100K of his money, and I began trading. At first the jitters were so intense I could barely control my own fingers. I was dizzy when I did the first trade. And I was super pumped when it turned out profitable. Within a week the account was already up to $105,000, and I was feeling a little less terrified. But one fine day, just when I thought everything was peachy keen, the trade I attempted was an incorrect buy signal. It hardly matched the criteria I had named. But I froze as the share price of the stock dropped . . . and dropped while I continued to hold the call options contracts. Normally, I would have bailed by this point, but I didn't. The sheer magnitude of loss within moments, which was minus $10,000, was so high that I felt like selling it would confirm that big of a loss, and that was something I couldn't fathom. Looking back on it, of course, losing $10,000 would have brought the account down from $105K to $95K. This would have been mildly disappointing, but far from devastating.

I remember thinking, "That's too big a loss, I can't sell, I need to wait for it to go back up." I sat there and started praying to every god in the universe to reverse the direction of the stock price and have it head back up. But if there are such gods, they must have known me to be a cheap charlatan and that my new-found love for them was a form of desperation rather than true faith. I may have even attempted a rain dance. None of these worked. The price plummeted. Hours had gone by, and the price kept rising a little, providing hope, and then dropping again, further than the last bottom. I wondered if my friend had checked the account. Should I call him? I've just lost tens of thousands of dollars of his money. We were down $20,000, and it didn't seem like the stock ever planned to go back up.

I decided to wait overnight, and when I woke up the following day (it was hard to sleep), the account was further down, at minus $25,000. I concluded that it would never stop dropping, and the best way to recover the lost money was to sell the calls and buy puts instead. This was a way I could capitalize on the down trend.

Puts are simply a type of option that allows you to make money when the stock is dropping rather than rising. You may have heard of "shorting" a stock. This is a similar concept in that you are betting on a stock dropping rather than on a stock rising and profiting from that.

I bought a pile of puts. This was a particular moment in my life where I realized that I was not inherently lucky. There were lucky people in this world. My younger brother was an example. He was obviously inherently lucky. Not everything always went his way, but at least sometimes! When chance was the deciding factor in my life, I lost. That was a near guarantee. This is why outsmarting my bad luck was and still is the best strategy. But for my younger brother, chance seemed to favor him.

Moments after I bought the puts, the stock decided it was completely done dropping and rose back up. As it rose, the account dropped from 75K to 65K to 55K.

There I was with the regret of selling the call options, which would have recovered if I had waited a little longer, piled on top of the compressing guilt of buying puts.

At no point did I ever discuss with my friend that I could hold on for days, trying out whatever I could, essentially gambling his money.

At this point I was not only a gambler, a religious charlatan, heretic or whatever, I was breaking my deal to my friend, withholding the state of affairs; I was a wreck. I try to be an honorable person. I don't cheat on my wife, I don't use illicit drugs, I don't text and drive, I don't lie unless it's some meaningless unimportant thing. But here I am being a full-on criminal. I broke bad.

I looked in the mirror and said atrocious things to myself. I had rarely if ever experienced such stress and self-crushing thoughts. I finally called my friend and told him the whole story. I then told him I wanted out of the joint account game. And that I would pay him back everything I lost. This added up to the same amount that I had stashed in my account for having the financial stability to raise a family. In a matter of two days, I reversed the books from positive to negative in the ledger of my life.

The friend was really cool, and did not expect it right away. He recognized that he had pressured me into a situation that was new and unusual, and he gave me plenty of time to come up with the money. What a relief. I have since paid him back, by the way. Every penny I lost. Even though the agreement was that I could lose a bunch and he wouldn't care. I felt like I broke the agreement by violating the system.

For weeks I felt like a phony, a loser, and I considered quitting the 20-Minute Trader gig altogether. How could I act like a badass, know-it-all when I was, by evidence, a bona fide, signed-and-sealed, museum-piece, dyed-in-the-wool, certified, USDA organic, LAY-HOO-ZA-HER?!

I called up one of the original 20-Minute Traders, Camilla, who has a knack for listening and understanding. I told her the whole story in detail. She understood the system well so I felt a keen understanding emanating from her.

"I'm a faker. These students of mine that are using my system think I am profitable, but I am not," I said.

"Okay. I get that," she said. "If you had applied your system correctly, how much would you have lost on that trade?"

"Four thousand five hundred dollars," I said.

"Okay, do the math. What would the account be at in that case?"

I went through and added up how much I was up doing 20-Minute Trading by the book. If you include my own winnings from my other accounts, as well as his, it was tens of thousands of dollars.

"The trade you did actually had nothing to do with your system. It was a desperate gamble," she said.

"Good point," I said.

"I have made so many thousands of dollars through your system. I have also lost money doing a bunch of experimental unrelated things," she said. "And it would be unfair for me to blame your system on my wild, non-standard trades."

I regrouped and put my technician hat back on, and carried on using the method in its purity.

And I did well again.

As 2021 rolled on, the number of requests to learn my strategy grew. I tried my best to communicate it all with my videos and over the phone, but it was simply too many people to work with.

A group of students got together and asked me to do a live seminar-style course over a weekend to teach the method and answer questions in a group setting. In March 2021, around 30 people showed up at an office space in Pasadena, California, the very city in which I discovered the original pattern.

Saturday and Sunday we went over basics, details about patterns, and looking at dozens of pattern video replays, to really get familiar with how it ought to look when doing real-time trades. On Monday morning, we met up again and were able to play around with paper trades when the market was actually open.

This was a chance to get everyone nimble with the buys and sells, and with seeing the charts move against real transactions and figures.

The course was a hit! Luckily, I hired a three-camera videographer team to capture the entire three days with high-def, great quality footage. We packaged the whole thing into a 55-lesson class called the "Secret Pattern Master Class."

You might be wondering, "Hey Jeremy, how come you are not telling us what ticker you discovered the pattern on?"

Well, to be honest, I am afraid that too many people knowing it could undo its efficacy. There are only so many options contracts for sale. If there are thousands of people trying to buy the same contracts at the same time, there won't be any available to buy and sell!

It could get saturated with too many players. This private Secret Pattern beach remains exclusive for us, so it avoids crowding and does not lose its charm!!!

This course is for sale on my website and is called the Secret Pattern Master Class. It even involves an NDA that one must sign upon starting it.

But I hold back nothing in that course. And to this day it's the most popular service that 20-Minute Trader offers.

A month or so after that live master class, I began to wonder if there was another pattern out there that I should be paying attention to.

I recalled that in my general browsing, I noted a pattern in a particular ticker, but never pursued it. Why would I? I had this well-oiled machine churning out money with my original one. Why waste my time exploring others?

What kicked me over the edge was the number of 20-Minute Traders who had not signed up for the master class and were asking for some pattern details and more direction on a ticker to choose. I decided to invest time into researching another ticker.

In May 2021, two months after I delivered that live course, I changed the ticker code from my usual one to the new one I suspected had a good pattern on it. The market opened. I had the Dow Jones on there as well. Both lines wormed across the screen, interacting like the double helix of a DNA molecule. After a few minutes, I saw the Dow Jones take a nice sharp, random and independent upturn. Then, like an obedient sidekick, the stock ticker shot up in response. It was twice as clear as the one I had been using for the past year and a half.

This stock zigged and zagged along the chart. When I looked into it, I found that this particular ticker also had the advantage of a significantly higher number of options contracts for sale, as compared to the other ticker I had been using. Which meant that I could scale up to even higher levels if I wanted to. I could get my account to where I am trading a million dollars a day with it and the volume of contracts being traded would easily be able to sustain that. This ticker was better than the one I had been using. Plain and simple.

I decided I would dedicate my time to going deeper and researching this thing down to its molecular level. I was going to go full rainman, geeking out about lines and charts and points and cents.

For this project, I garnered the assistance of 30 beta testers. As luck would have it, in May and the first part of June, this ticker was so easy to make money on that all of us were successfully guessing buy points that profited. We simply assumed that the price would zig and zag. Zig would be the upward motion and zag would be the downward motion. If the price showed us a zag (down), and the Dow started to zig, we would buy, and the ticker would rise into a zig (up), and we would profit. We thought we had the easiest hack in history and couldn't believe it.

The end of June was humbling, though. It was clear there was more here than meets the eye. We spent the rest of the summer attempting to identify what specific criteria gave us the highest likelihood of a follow-up rise of the share price. I received daily feedback from each beta tester, finding out what obstacles, buy points, indicators, predictors, and successful actions we found. I tabulated and relooked, tested, and challenged everything.

By the end of the summer, I had a variety of criteria sets that seemed to plausibly predict a small rally with a decent amount of reliability and ruggedness. But that was not even close to what I needed to create the perfect system. And when I say "criteria," I mean the values of time, points, cents, or trends of these lines and the exacting quantities to look for when trying to predict a rise. I wanted total objectivity with no need for a knack, a feeling, or a hunch. I wanted one set of criteria or parameters that was so precise it could be written into code and used instead of having a human determine and interpret. That was the end goal—total automation. And this end goal would get us furthest along in manual trading. We wanted a specific action response to each situation, so in the moment, there was never a question of what to do. There was always a right answer for what to do if A happens or if B happens.

I had been working with a software team to build a back tester that appeared identical to TradingView in its presentation of one-second information but could be fed data from the past and, in essence, simulate the market back then.

TradingView data does not allow one to go back very far with its one-second charts, perhaps a day or so. I needed to go back weeks, months, and years to test out these criteria and see which set held up the longest and which set could be relied upon to last into the future. These charts would have to have the ability to self-scale automatically as we zoomed in and out rather than flying off the top or bottom of the chart, give us exact values at each point, and show the interrelationship between the Dow Jones and the ticker. In order to create this time machine we simply needed a flux capacitor and a DeLorean . . . oh wait, that was another project. We needed the values of the Dow Jones and the ticker for every second of the market for every day of trading over the span of three years.

This was 46 million values. We purchased this information from the exchange.

I began my time travel back to January 2018, choosing the first trading day of the year. I looked over the chart and used the criteria of the first set I had hypothesized might be the one that would best predict. I saw each parameter one after the other. Right after these criteria manifested, the stock ticker rose nicely, by 25 cents. This certainly would have been a profitable trade. I looked over the span of the entire 20 minutes for any other times this specific set of criteria manifested, looked to see, as well, if there was a follow-up rally, or if the stock dropped instead. I noted these details on my worksheet. I even included when these occurred down to the precise second. I looked at how much the stock jumped and how much it traveled downward before eventually jumping. This was so I knew how much cushion I should provide. In other words, how far down should I allow the stock price to drop before I expected to see it rise and profit? Since it is not always the case that there is an immediate rally upon buying, it can happen that the rally comes 45 seconds after the criteria presented itself. Perhaps the stock ticker share price line on my chart would drift down a bit first. Calculating the number of cents it tended to drop at the most, at the least, and on average would give me sell criteria. These data would tell me when to cut my losses and when to hold on for the rally.

I then checked the next set of criteria that we had hypothesized over the same 20-minute period of the same day, tabulating the same specifics. I did the same with the next set of criteria for that one day. It took me 35 minutes to properly calculate all these figures. I then went on to the second day and did the same tabulations. I repeated this multiple-set-test exercise for the majority of the next 900 trading days up until August 2021. I spent considerable time daily staring at these charts and tables. Tedious time very well spent.

At the end of it, I found the winning set.

If one had simply identified four simple criteria, things like, "The Dow Jones does an unsynchronized rally of 18 points," as well as making sure five *Trade Stoppers* were not present, which included things like, "If the ticker just dropped by over 45 cents avoid buying for the next minute," then that trader would have 92% winning trades between January 2, 2018 and September 1, 2021.

This was a truly remarkable breakthrough.

I had also identified the lowest expectable rise value of the ticker and knew how much value to request when the ticker responded with a rally. I also concluded how far down the ticker's share price might go, knew it had gone below the expectable small drop that often preceded the rally, and if the value went below that point, I could bail with a loss and not suffer a worse loss.

We had the winning formula, and it was now time to use it.

My son, Owen Asher Russell, was born September 5, 2021 at Cedars Sinai hospital in Los Angeles, California.

Naturally, this dominated my time for the next couple of weeks while the beta testers munched on these new yummy criteria. We enjoyed the reliability, preciseness, and ruggedness of this set of parameters as it produced constant successful buy signals resulting in rallies of the share price.

You may be wondering now, "But what are these parameters?"

I must emphasize again that I would be an idiot to publish these details as the overuse of the exact same ticker and buy point would saturate the buying and selling of the contracts that I and a few others use. You may gain access to this information if you become part of a tribe who subscribe to what we call at this time, "God Mode."

God Mode is currently the most advanced service that 20-Minute Trader offers when it comes to manual trading of a buy signal. Inquiries about this can be made on the website 20mintrader.com.

By the time I had settled in with the newest member of our family, I was back at it, and the beta testers and I were playing this pattern daily.

Around this time, I discovered the point of folly that infected every trader on the team. The same element I have described several times throughout this book, in which the trader is tempted to hope and hold rather than exit on a small loss.

Traders would use the pattern to make wonderful profits, and then would wipe out large chunks of these profits by hoping and holding on a failed signal as their accounts depleted by large chunks.

I did pep talks on a regular basis to attempt to discourage this practice. It is as if these traders were hypnotized into hoping and holding and simply could not stop themselves.

As I said previously, but will say again, I decided to make a game out of it. Anyone who could go for a whole month without hoping and holding on any losing trade would win a grand prize of several thousand dollars.

Immediately, 20 people entered this game. After only a week and half, 10 had disqualified themselves by failing to sell on a small loss, but rather holding on for it to rise back up. A week later—another 5. They were dropping like flies even with the reward of cash within grasp. These people were swayed by the devil on their shoulders. I finally started calling the last 5 remaining players daily, before the market opened, and had to practically threaten them (bribing apparently wasn't working). In the last week or so, another still failed and only 4 remained pure to the game.

All 4 of those players greatly outperformed the others and had significant profits to show for it.

I didn't look upon these disqualified players with disdain or disgust. I looked at them only as I did myself. Since I too had been a major violator, having wiped out months of profit with a single hope-and-hold on several occasions. But I was conclusively convinced that no one was immune to this disease.

The year 2021 wrapped up with stellar heights achieved in the markets. But I was super suspicious. I looked at the NASDAQ chart over the past ten years and noted that in four years, its value had nearly tripled. Meanwhile, the rest of the world's prices had not tripled in that same period. Maybe some things but not most. I was wary and leery. I knew we had a crash coming. These were unsustainable heights. It was like the market was high on meth about ready to come down. My system had held well in 2021 . . . but whose didn't? Everything was flying up. Anything you flung out would stick. Gurus were raking in dough for their "excellent" strategies. I wondered if mine too depended upon a bullish market. Was I a fake? Would my system work in a bear market?

In January 2022, I funded an account with $8,000 and began using my strategy exactly according to Hoyle. If you don't know what "according to Hoyle" is, you may not be a card player. "According to Hoyle" is an expression meaning "exactly per the rules." Hoyle was the book card players referred to when there was ever a question about the rules of play. They would say, "That's not according to Hoyle," if some schmo was trying to do something unusual.

Well, I played my own rules according to Hoyle. And by February 11 of that year, while the market decided to take a full-on deep nose-dive, my account was at $16,000. Doubled in just over a month. Gains like these continued and I certainly enjoyed them. I don't even recall how high my gains got by March, but they were impressive, especially in a bear market.

Until one fine day in early March I decided to think myself invincible, and not sell when the stock dropped down. Instead, I held on and even added in more, hoping for a comeback. And all my gains were gone just like that. Luckily, I had been pulling out winnings along the way, so the burn was soothed slightly.

What is amazing about the stock market is its timing. It seems to know exactly when you will feel most certain and most confident. Exactly when you will let your guard down and go easy on your discipline. It truly fattens you up like a pig in a slaughterhouse, letting you indulge like you are a king. After months of success and constant good luck, the only logical conclusion you could make is that you are special. You are different from everyone else. The statistics prove it conclusively. You have a touch and a knack, and no one can strike you down. Things always go in your favor.

Right when you are done patting yourself on the back, your arm gets grabbed and amputated savagely at the shoulder. It's a shocker and leaves you stunned, bleeding out.

Right around that same time, I went on a short trip to San Francisco to see my family. I was hanging out with them, having dinners and playing games. It was really fun.

On the third day there, I was sitting in my mother's living room and my wife called from Los Angeles.

"Hello?"

"Hey, Jeremy some guy just tried to break into the house!"

Jessica and Owen had been home alone in Van Nuys, California, a sketchy part of LA, with no car in the driveway, which tells the would-be burglar that no one is home.

"What?? Are you okay? What happened?"

"I was in the living room playing with Owen, and some man started shaking the doorknob and messing with the lock. I could see his outline through the fogged windows in the door."

"Did you yell out at him?" I asked.

"No, I froze and then ran into the bedroom with Owen and locked the door then the bathroom door and called the police. They showed up pretty fast but by then the guy was gone."

"Holy crap!"

"I gave the cops the details and they are on the lookout."

"Did they look at our security footage?"

"No, all cameras had run out of battery," she said.

I had failed to charge the batteries of the cameras. When I lost all the money in the market, I had gone into a bit of a daze and neglected some key duties. I had always kept these cameras operational. They require charging every month or two, and I even get alerted to charge the batteries when they are low.

But in my stupor of shock, I had failed to act on these alerts. I put my family in peril as a result.

It was 8 p.m. by the time she called, and I couldn't get down there to LA in less than seven hours.

I called my dad immediately. He lived 20 minutes away and is ex-military, a vet. I told him the whole story, asked him if he could stay overnight, and that I would return in the morning. Without hesitation he agreed, and got some gear and headed over.

I got home in the early afternoon. I looked at the crime reports for our area. Not good overall. In fact, the month before, we could see our house from a news helicopter following fugitives that were hopping my neighbor's fences. They got within yards of our house as they fled, breaking into houses along the way. I could see my barbecue on the live news channel, with spotlights searching for the suspects.

We often received notifications about criminal activity near us. Things like, "body found in trunk of car 350 feet away," and so on.

"We need to get the hell out of this neighborhood right away," said Jessica.

"No kidding," I replied.

That very day I went on the hunt for better places to live. Sure enough, there were places only 20 minutes away that had incredibly low crime and which were clean and nice. LA is one of the most diverse places you could ever imagine, and I don't just mean ethnically. I mean every category. You can tell which part of LA someone lives in by their accent. Everyone has heard of a "valley girl." That's because girls who lived in the Valley of LA sound a certain and classifiable way. But if you go to Santa Monica, people sound more like Bill and Ted.

And, of course, most of my friends growing up were not white Anglo-Saxon Protestant or Catholic. They were Mexican, Black, Asian, Jewish, Middle Eastern, Russian, Indian, and so on.

Nice, safe places were three times the rent of the house we were in at that time, even though it was only 20 minutes away.

I did some math and found out that mortgage payments would be cheaper than rent and would help us build equity. Of course, I would need the down payment, but still.

I went on the hunt to buy.

I had to empty every account I had for anything anywhere so that I could have the bank statements I needed to show I could manage buying a house. I scraped and earned and traded and did everything I could to get the cash together to make this home ownership dream a reality. And I was desperate to get it done immediately. To get my family safe at a nice home in a safe area. I also wanted the ability to modify the home into one we loved. This meant we had to buy.

We drove around looking at houses all over town. We found several that really fit the bill. Room for me to work from home, have a nice backyard, good playing space for Owen. We tried putting up offers for a couple but they were snatched up right away. It was the time when houses were posted for sale and gone within a day or two. House after house disappeared off the market. This was right about the time when interest rates were hiking up on a monthly basis, so everyone who wanted to move was selling and buying like it was Black Friday. We found a home we loved in an amazing neighborhood and put in a bid. We were so excited about this one that we started really imagining what it would be like to live there. It even had a pool and an office separated from the house, which is ideal for me.

We started envisioning the renovations we were going to do, and all the furniture we would get.

But we lost it to someone else. We were particularly disheartened. A few days later, we were driving through another magical neighborhood, even better than the one we lost. There were no cars on the road, an extreme rarity in LA. Instead, squirrels played in the streets and scattered as we drove up, plush lawns, 70-foot trees, and kids playing in the yards. Then, we saw something we never thought we'd see in a central part of Los Angeles. Walking right down the middle of the road were two beautiful horses, one black, one white, carrying their owners along. It turns out this neighborhood was zoned for equestrian dwelling.

Each house was its own little magical creation rather than a clone of all the others. As we parked, a lovely lady with a little black dog greeted us, as she threw a tennis ball right into the street, and the little puppy fetched it.

What kind of Truman show, Brady bunch, Twilight Zone had we entered? Was this still LA? Where are the sirens? The traffic? The criminals?

And let's be clear, this place was centralized, right in the heart of hearts of LA, but somehow in its own little world.

We went hard to bid for this house and we got it, even though we way overpaid and I was completely and utterly broke by the time I had the place paid for and all fees and moving costs done. Every credit card was maxed, and the bank account was close to empty. But I kept one thing in place. I had 50K in my trading account. And trading this was going to have to cover life expenses.

Starting in June 2022, I began an even more systematic approach to my trading method. Every Monday morning, I pulled out every penny I had made above the $50K principal. Sometimes that would be $3,000, sometimes $2,500, sometimes $3,500. I would start the Monday trading day at $50,000 even. I would do my exact strategy every morning, all within the first 20 minutes of market open, and that would be it for trading that day. All in all, it averaged around $11,500 of profit per month. This covered exactly what we needed for the mortgage, food, utilities, back bills on the cards, car, gas, and that's about it. I really couldn't get away with fooling around with the method. I couldn't gamble. I had to be exacting and standard since I needed this money to live. By the end of August, I had pulled out over $30,000 that got us through the summer.

However, yet again, I fell prey to the hope and hold demon, and lost a sizeable chunk, all in one stupid move in which I failed to bail a small loss.

If I recall correctly, I lost $22,000. Forgive me if the memory is both super clear, precise, fuzzy, and forgettable at the same time.

It was a devastating setback. The crazy thing is that I was so disciplined for so many months, day after day, never faltering. And all it took was one moment of falter and the house of cards got blown down.

I am just glad I was taking out money constantly, because if I hadn't been, the loss could have been so much greater.

One of the biggest problems with trading in general is that the system lends itself and has appeal to risk takers, gamblers, pirates, free spirits, geniuses, and innovators. And yet the role that wins the most is the timid nerd; the steady, systematic trader; the ritualist; the technician; the researcher.

The adventurer will nearly always come to grief, unless they happen to be one of the lucky ones who hits it so big, the sheer size of the win overshadows any losses or setbacks. But even with these cats, the number of those who blow their loot is rather astonishing.

One of these risk-taking maniacs was that good friend of mine I mentioned earlier who lost so much so fast. He had made a good batch of cash running businesses and by the age of 28 was a millionaire. But he was a millionaire from two sources. One was his business that made him hundreds of thousands of extra dollars of spending cash, and the other source was his aggressive and successful investments into crypto assets. Keep in mind though, there were times he was down $500,000 and had to come up with extra money to keep his margin from being called. It wasn't like he chose a coin, bought it, it shot up like a rocket, and he sold it like any other lottery winner. No, he had to endure the pain of extreme setbacks and the pain of holding on and having faith in his bet.

By May 2022, his personal net worth had grown to $8 million.

He started posting things on social media about being financially free, but I thought the angle he took was bad karma. I remember thinking while reading it, "Bro, this angle is bound to piss off the universe and catch you out." He was doing frequent social media posts about how a 9-to-5 job was slavery and a grind and that going to college was a waste of time and unnecessary. The flavor was mildly condescending to people who work 9 to 5. In my opinion, these viewpoints are false and even hostile to mostly great people. First of all, 9-to-5 jobs people keep the world turning. He is able to drive the car he drives, use the phone he uses, and wear the shoes he wears because of those wage earners working, building, manufacturing, managing and creating these products. His warehouse employees were also working 9-to-5 jobs for his company to do Amazon sales. Does he see his own employees as lesser people? He depends on them. To say that someone is inferior because they work 9 to 5 is both not true and arrogant. Secondly, college graduates are the same engineers that built the roads and bridges he drives his Porsche on, the doctors that kept his mother alive for another couple of years, and the architects that designed his condo on the water. They are all losers? I didn't like his stance on these issues; they came across as "superior" to hard-working and laudatory individuals. I started communicating this to him where I could so he would have my opinion, since I otherwise loved the guy.

One day in May 2022 he called me.

"Jeremy! I just lost all of my money!" he said frantically.

"What do you mean all of it?" I asked.

"I lost $8 million overnight."

"How?" I asked.

"I had everything in Luna." The crypto coin.

"Everything?" I asked.

"Yes, all but the small amount of money I keep in my personal bank accounts."

This fellow had bet his entire life on this coin, and one day it disappeared into the ether. He never pulled out a million to save, he never diversified his investments over multiple streams, he simply went all in on this one asset.

"Two of my friends just offed themselves, they lost even more," he said. "And I've never felt so bad in my whole life. . . ."

I got the unmistakable idea that he was thinking about this as well.

"Listen!!" I said. "You are an inspiration to thousands of people. We all watched you become a millionaire in no time. You made us believe we could do it too! Now, all eyes are on you! If you turn this around and become a millionaire again, you'll change the lives of thousands of people who know and look up to you. And you CAN do it! You already did it once, and you can do it again!"

"Really?"

"No doubt!" I exclaimed.

For the next three weeks I talked to him regularly, getting updates on how he was doing. Keeping him motivated. As I write this one year later, he has since been able to build a new company and has managed his personal finances to a point where he is heading back to the baller position. He has also become humble and more grounded. And he certainly taught me, through his situation, how important risk management is as well as taking out winnings and placing them in a safe spot.

After that $22K loss, I regrouped and got my basic strategy back under control. But overall, I was running down on trading. Not because my 20-Minute Trader strategy was failing me but because not only did I do these 20-minute trades, I also did swing trades. These are trades that last over days or weeks, and for some reason, I have never been good at this. In fact, I have lost large amounts of money doing this repeatedly. If it wasn't for 20-Minute Trader trades making me so much, I would have been tens of thousands of dollars in the hole.

To give you an example of a swing trade, this is where I buy 100 call options contracts that expire in two weeks in the hopes that within the next few days, the underlying stock would rise by some amount. Then, as the days elapse, the price does not go up, but the call options depreciate through decay. Finally, the value of the position I bought into becomes so worthless the only thing I can do is sell it for pennies on the dollar. If the price had risen, I would have profited.

This can be bested as a technique, I am sure, but for the most part I truly and evidently stink at it. And I didn't know why I continued to attempt it. But it has been the main thing that has erased my 20-Minute Trader gains.

Nonetheless, the technique with which I was 20-minute trading continued to work like magic so I decided to take on really teaching people exactly how it is done. Again, I am not a financial advisor so I was able to simply write a curriculum and publish it rather than give individual advice, but then I spent considerable time ensuring that each understood every exact step. I carefully went through their chart settings, their broker account settings, paper traded buys, and sells until their fingers were blistered, and they didn't even have to think about it.

Sixteen people trained on this method. And after I did my best to educate, ten did well, while six were losing money, despite my attempts to make them competent and confident. Of the ten that were profiting, I am putting in a legal disclaimer here that I did not get their broker statements or screenshots, but they claimed to have been profiting at that time, and I believed them. The failing group was, of course, something that kept me up at night. I wanted 100% success with my students, but I wasn't even close to that. Why were these people failing at my system when it was so clear and so easy?

It was so tested, back-tested, rigorously employed over long periods of time, and appeared to be ruggedly reliable. Yet these six people kept reporting continued losses.

I decided to deep dive into this and find out what was happening.

As I mentioned earlier in this book, some were Californians that didn't like waking up early. They weren't as sharp at 6:15 a.m. as they may have been at other times of the day. But even so, this system should work no matter your state, was my thought.

A more important common denominator among the "losers" was their lack of exacting certainty and confidence on what to do in each and every scenario. It would be like if you were driving a car, and the vehicle in front of you stopped, and you had to look up in a manual what to do in the event that a car in front of you halted. Then you say, "Ah yes, apply the brake . . . now where is that again?" BOOM!! Crash.

This is the type of thing that my students were running into. Not knowing the one exact right move to do in every scenario instantly.

In 20-Minute Trader technique, seconds make a big difference. Things are FAST and happen in short frantic bursts. Buy then sell. Boom, boom.

Hesitation is deadly.

I created a set of drills for these "losers." I gave them multiple trade scenarios with exact details and asked them what to do in each one. For example, I would say, you see the Dow Jones drop along with the stock you are trading for a period of ten seconds in sync, what do you do next? And if the student did not answer right away with, "Look for a divergent Dow motion," I would give them the correct answer and drill it again. Then I would say, "You see the divergent Dow motion upward, what to do next?" and they would have to say, "Buy the option contract." In essence this type of drilling would go on with hundreds of questions until the student knew the exact right answer for pretty much every scenario that could be encountered. This type of innovative drilling resulted in completely competent players, like I had never seen before. And they reported doing very well on their earnings (again I cannot corroborate their claims with broker statements but I can say that they made these claims, and I had no reason to disbelieve them).

Since then, I have trained specialists who were themselves successful traders in this method, and have taken on more students. I keep the number relatively low so I can work with people personally as needed, since too many people could spread me so thin I would not be available for any one person for longer than minutes.

These people sign NDAs as well, so as not to leak the intellectual property of this method and cause saturation that would render it useless.

I am going to give you my trading update within this chapter.

As I said in the earlier one, on May 15, 2023, I decided to go bigger on my trading and teamed up with a wealthy friend, creating a new joint account with exactly $800,000 in it. I began trading this account that very day and my first trade was a profit of $5,535.21. By the end of the week, I had added $13,299.17 to the account value.

I must say, the fear juice that coursed through my veins in that first week was so intense, I ended each session with the shakes. Who knows what internal hormones and chemicals were released in the process. For one thing, I don't normally have armpit odor per se, but I am embarrassed to admit that I had to change my shirt right after due to whatever repelling substances my body felt the need to emit when under that kind of acute stress. But after a few weeks, my nerves had cooled, and I was able to maintain some form of equanimity while trading.

By June 6, the account value had grown to $875,913.70. This was due to simply doing my daily 20-minute trades, but with more money than I had ever traded with before.

As described in my last trading update, I had that crazy loss and recovery from early June to late July. I am going to retell part of it here.

The joint investor called me in the middle of the debacle.

"What's going on, Jer?" he asked.

"I completely screwed up. And we are way in the hole."

"How?" he asked. I told him the whole story, and I also told him how I intended to resolve it. He was willing to let me try to recover the money in a very risky way. But only if I was willing to pay back the losses from my super non-standard actions. I agreed to this. I deployed my recovery strategy, and ended up losing only $67,000 on that trade, as I had described. I can say "only" because I was down so much more, that this was fantastic news comparatively. I also pledged to never ever fail to place a stop loss ever again, and if I did fail to do so, there would be consequences. My friend was a kind soul, and never tried to run me down for this, but accepted my promises knowing they would help me prevent such an intense mishap again.

Over the next week of trading, I tried to recover the lost profits, and in doing so, I lost another $64,000, and the account was down to $756K. I was about to throw in the towel, call the publisher of this book, and tell them that I am not fit to write something like this. My fellow joint account holder again reassured me that he was not mad, and he supported me in my endeavors to make this work. He told me not to give up.

Then there was the other friend who called me, a trader whom I had taught and who was making great money at my strategy.

"Stop trying to make it all back in one trade," he said. And as I said before, his words were completely correct. Yes, the first trade that lost $67,000 was painful, so painful. But my strategy is very simple. Predict a tiny jump and claim the profit connected with that specific tiny jump. End of story. What I had been trying to do was hold on longer than the expectable rise, hoping it would rise even more. When it failed to, it would drop and my stop loss would get activated.

As I said in the update, I took my trader friend's advice and began from scratch little by little, rebuilding the account using only standard little trades. By July 3, I was back above the principal value at $802,689.11.

July was a great month, and by the end of it, the account value had risen to $933,103.11. I was up over $133K from the principal amount, despite having been down by $44,000 six weeks earlier. That includes the fact the I had multiple trades that lost over $12,000 when I got stopped out on a stop loss.

From this experience I learned two valuable lessons. The first is the one I showcase the most in this book and in all my writings on trading, "Always use a stop loss on every trade you do." The second lesson was to "Not try to make it all back in one trade."

As I write this sentence on August 22, the account value is $1,022,677.31. It is up $222,677.31 from the initial investment amount of $800,000 from three months earlier.

Chapter 22
All That 20-Minute Trader Offers

Now, I am talking to you as someone who has cracked a code and has brokerage statements to prove it. But this was not because I am a lucky person, or someone with the Midas touch. I have also successfully taught this method to a lot of people.

If someone wanted to read this book and then go about finding a pattern, doing the research connected with making it reliable, and having a system with the goal of granting them a side income that takes as much time daily to execute as it does to wait for a smoothie at an Erewon store, they could do so. All the answers in every detail are covered here in. Erewon is a California grocery store known for hipster snob vibes.

You would have to choose a stock, make sure it's uptrending over years, follow the steps of discovering a pattern, which really comes down to quality journaling and note taking, and then play around with it until the parameters of the buy signal and the specifics of the sell strategy are definable.

You would have to make note of these and follow them, taking care not to use important money, learn about and use stop losses, and be patient and scientific.

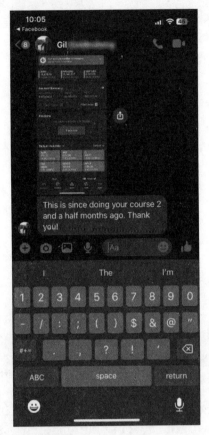

FIGURE 22.1

A gentleman named Gil messaged me yesterday. This was the screenshot. You can see his profit is over $65,000.

For legal I must disclaim, I am not claiming this screenshot as factual. I have not looked at his trading and broker statements. This could be fabricated by him in photoshop or something. But I do attest here that I simply screenshot this message while I was writing this and posted it on this page. I have many of these.

I would be remiss if I failed to describe the services that we have at 20mintrader.com. None of these services are needed. You have everything you need in the book. But I will describe them in case you want to know about them. Note, as the months and years go by, some of these services change in terms of name and/or content. But as of this writing and for the foreseeable future, these are what we have.

The 20-Minute Trader Free Course

The service explains the system in its entirety, outlining the style, research methodology, a description of the stock market and options for dummies, and how you could derive the whole strategy from scratch. However, it does not provide specifics on what buttons to push precisely. It is under 15 minutes long.

The Predictable Trading Bundle

This service includes 3.5 hours of video content that carefully defines the concepts and curated key words you will need to know. It spells out how the stock market works and what options are. It walks you through the whole setup of their charts and how to use them.

It illustrates how to properly set up the brokerage account and how to trade on it. The course provides a visual and descriptive walkthrough of how to discover a pattern, as outlined in this book, but in video form. It discusses how to try and capitalize on a predictable pattern while providing tips for success and avoiding major mishaps. It is the least expensive service we offer for sale, yet it is comprehensive.

The Secret Pattern Master Class

For the 20-Minute Trader, this is the highest tier of expertise offered of all its online services. It reveals the ticker I used, the actual pattern I discovered initially, and comprehensive details of the criteria with dozens of videos showing it in action. During my live master class in front of a room full of people in Pasadena, California, I had a three-camera videography team capture the whole thing while I wore a high-quality mic. The key element in this class is the videos of the pattern in action. Over the month before the live course, I recorded the moving charts of the pattern itself while narrating what I was looking for and how I was able to use these motions to predict this particular stock rise. I outlined the criteria I had identified for maximum success in being right about it while detailing the exacting exit strategy I had found most workable, both on the profit and loss sides. It is over 50 lessons and almost nine hours of content, over three hours of simply showing pattern after pattern in motion. Currently, the majority of the positive reviews connected with 20-Minute Trader® are from those doing this Secret Pattern Master Class service.

Elite Trading Club

This club has become the overall favored service for participants in 20-Minute Trader® education. In any field, most people need direction and guidance—an expert to assist them along the way. The club gives them unlimited access to a 20-Minute Trader® expert for setting up charts, brokerage settings, getting questions answered about the service they are on, help in identifying patterns, and using them to profit. It provides a community of like-minded traders to share their thoughts, experiences, trades, ask questions, get info, and form friendships. At this time, the club provides a widget that can easily be plugged into your chart showing when an index has risen by a certain amount, which helps identify possible buy signals without the need to calculate small details on the fly. It has a "text-in-your-trade" service that the participant can send in the time of their trade, and an expert will look at it and send feedback on how well this buy signal adhered to the basic rules and criteria for pattern spotting. It is an evaluation and analysis service, like an internship, for predictable pattern identification and is one-on-one. No financial advice is offered whatsoever. Coaches only teach or refer to the published works. Lastly, I do a bi-monthly Q and A with all members in a live-streaming experience that allows specific questions to be answered immediately.

Bulletproof Strategy

This is an add-on that everyone in every trading strategy needs. However, you should note that the entirety of that video course is in this book, and you have already studied it. Those who want to watch the video version of it can find it on the website 20mintrader.com. It is how to mitigate, prevent, and deal with losses in trading. This course has a method to help you gain the qualities that optimize maximum performance found nowhere else in any system anywhere other than these pages. It is an entirely unique technique to help establish best practices in the field of trading. Bulletproof strategy is a stand-alone service, but anyone on any 20-Minute Trader service should study this for a better chance at long-term success.

God Mode

The term God Mode is used in video game parlance to mean "invincible" and "omni-resourceful." The player in God mode cannot die and never runs out of resources. I haven't played video games in a long time, but the term is borrowed from that activity because that's how I felt when I discovered the pattern I use today. I have already described this service in detail but I will outline the basic features here. Note: This service is exclusive and openings are limited; however, there is a waitlist. I work with the person one-on-one but not in an advice capacity. I am not an advisor; I am an educator, plain and simple. I teach everyone in the God Mode community the exact same published strategy, and I do not provide individual advice to anyone. The criteria for the God Mode pattern were painstakingly back-tested with both software algorithms and manual sanity checks until the detailed values of each parameter were a distilled masterpiece of simplicity. There are four things to look for on a buy signal, and five trade stoppers to be aware of, and they are clearly outlined in confidential video and written form for members of the God Mode community. When someone signs up for God Mode, they are granted one year of unlimited services with myself and my team of specialists, who provide white-glove concierge level support. Specifically, they place the student on a progress board and provide them with a checklist ensuring that each step is completed and accomplished before going on to the next. At first, the specialists make sure the student is well set up with their trading tools. Because I have a deal with the most popular brokerage for this system, I get huge discounts on fees for all God Mode students. This alone saves many thousands of dollars per year. We also ensure their chart setup is the simplest and most user-friendly way to perform the God Mode strategy and that they know how to use it. Then, they progress on the checklist into learning the method. These steps include studying the details of the pattern, watching videos demonstrating them, practicing each individual criterion, then all of them combined. It only allows participants to advance to the next levels by demonstrating understanding and expertise on the level they just completed. For example, it is vital that a God Mode trader can sell a position within 10 seconds of purchase. This requires a muscle-memory level of competence in using the trading app. Our specialists use paper trading to walk you through the buying and selling process—slowly at first and then faster and faster until they can complete the transaction in less than 12 seconds from start to finish, stopwatch and all (don't worry, there are no whistles). Then, they are allowed to progress on to the next step on the checklist. Competence is promised because it is inevitable. One cannot move on without demonstrating it. As a result, members that get through these steps are confident.

Every day, before market open I provide my own premarket thoughts, analysis, news, and how I intend to view the trading day. After the trading period has ended, I send in a screenshot of my trade, detailing how many contracts I purchased, what the strike price and expiry were, how much I paid for each contract, and the precise moments I bought and sold.

The student will send me their trade as well, and I will look at it on my chart to determine if they correctly called a buy signal with all necessary criteria present, and that there were no trade-stoppers when the purchase occurred.

God Mode students become friends, and I tend to stay in touch with them over time. Although God Mode is the "best pattern," this does not take away from other services that stand on their own as valuable and potentially workable ways to use predictable patterns to capitalize on small market movements.

It is no surprise that I would be innovating and spearheading the best possible ways to play this game and that better and better systems would evolve. Again, this does not discredit the earlier models. Just because my car is a 2017 model does not mean it fails to get me from point A to point B safely. I'm sure the latest model is wonderful, but it is not necessary per se.

As I said, this is the exclusive inner circle with waiting lists. If you want to inquire into God Mode, simply go onto 20mintrader.com, find the God Mode section, and click to book a call.

20-Minute Trader Bot

Lastly, I have been working on and finally started using a bot that replicates my God Mode trades. This project started in November 2020 when a student brought up the idea and started to pursue it. Over the next year, I worked with programmers to develop formulas that allowed the algorithm to see what I see and do what I do. After a year of work, we did not have anything really impressive, but at least we were able to build the back-tester in the process, and used this to optimize our parameters and criteria. But that is also when Robin came along and asked if he could help me build a bot, exclusive of the team I had been working with.

He had a master's degree in actuarial science, as well as a bachelor's in mathematics. He had traded futures for banks for ten years, using billions of dollars to leverage these instruments that are quite similar to options in many ways. He felt I had something special and wanted to invest time and effort in making it something automatic. Over the next year and a half, we made thousands of lines of code, creating formulas that attempted to replicate my actions precisely. Finally, in May 2023, the bot appeared ready for deployment.

We had tested it, retested it, did sanity checks, and every day we looked at the signals it chose, and almost all were accurate to what I had done the same day.

The sophistication involved in these formulas is astonishing and mind-boggling. I found myself using high school and college math I thought I would never use. Turning concepts into math formulas! Luckily, I loved math as a subject when I was younger, and actually understood most of it.

I recall a time in an Advanced Placement class in high school studying calculus. One day, the professor put a huge problem on the chalkboard and said that whoever could get this formula right the fastest would be permitted to leave class early. Right when he finished the last number on the equation, I raised my hand and said, "Four?"

The math professor flinched, "How did you know that?"

The truth is I didn't know. It turns out my guess was correct. But to properly analyze each part of the problem should take a super genius about ten minutes to get through. It ran all the way across the whole board, then to the next line across the board again.

Perhaps some of you recall the movie *Back to School* with Rodney Dangerfield. In that movie, he had to pass a math test, and when he was presented with a super-complicated problem, he sat there and just said, "Four?" And this was the moment he earned his diploma because he got it right. I was semi-jokingly doing the same thing Rodney's character did, and even imitated the inflection of his voice when I raised my hand and said it. But the professor was not very happy with my answer. He was 100% convinced I had been through his stuff and made notes on his problems and answers. He was certain I was a cheater, which he announced to the class. The funny thing, all of the other students knew me well, and knew that not only was I not a cheater, but was openly against the practice. And other students who may have cheated were giggling under their breath since I was famous for my anti-cheating policies. My response to the professor was, "I literally just guessed the answer! I was quoting *Back to School*!" I wasn't even upset at his accusation. I found it amusing especially because I knew not only was it decidedly untrue, but also that I could prove it in any setting.

He wasn't convinced. It was close to the end of the senior year and there was one final exam a few days later. He carefully selected a seat for me, which he had inspected with his own eyes and hands for tampering. This seat was jammed into the corner well away from the other students, against the far wall. Before I sat down, he asked me to empty my pockets and to keep my bag a distance from the desk. I happily complied. I let him know, "I know you think I went through your stuff and found math problems and answers, but I will prove to you in this test that I never cheated, and that I am actually against cheating as a matter of moral principle."

He seemed taken aback by this but proceeded to keep his plans in place, which I was happy about.

Mid-test, I needed an eraser but my bag was too far away. "Does anyone have an eraser I can borrow?"

"No!" he yelped. "I'll give you one." He provided me with the eraser, I completed the test before anyone else, and handed it in.

"You may go," he said, and I left the classroom.

Two days later, as we walked into class the professor said, "Jeremy, see me after class."

"Okay, Mr. Jacquard," I said.

"I need to announce something to the class," the professor started to say. "In the last few days, I have publicly stated I believed Jeremy to be a cheater. When I issued these tests to all of you, I changed Jeremy's test a little in case he was somehow getting answers from you. I kept the tests locked in a case that was never tampered with. I made sure of that. Jeremy then completed the test more than 30 minutes before everyone else in the class and got 100% of the questions right, plus the extra credit question worth another 10%. He got an A+. I retract all of my accusations, and I apologize for making them."

Everyone looked at me. I felt like I was being encouraged to gloat, and honestly, my demeanor at the time would have lent itself to that. Instead, I said, "It's fine. You had a valid reason to think so and I am glad you did that stuff to make sure I wasn't so I could prove it."

After class he said he wanted to meet me at a pizza place and buy me dinner, which we ended up doing a week or so later.

I love math as a tool for allowing one to solve and predict things that happen in real life, and I loved the challenge of figuring it out despite extreme complexities. This inclination has lent itself well to my current success in this method, and even more so with the bot.

After only one month, the bot, trading with real money, was at a 12.5% profit.

This bot is building a track record right now and will possibly be available for license sales by the time this book is released.

Each of these services is designed to assist you at your correct level. If someone asks me what the trading method is, I will naturally tell them that God Mode is the best since that is what I use. And that is not a fabrication. Those learning God Mode are told every detail of what I do and what I have discovered or continue to discover. But it is not cheap, and I don't expect anyone to jump on board with God Mode unless they have that kind of expendable cash since the number of hours that the specialists and I will be spending on them warrants such a fee. But it is not so expensive that ordinary people are denied access. I could probably sell it for $25,000 a pop, but then who could use it? Only wealthy people. And yet I purport to aid the working person who wants some extra income. If I charged that much, I'd be excluding too many folks. So, it is well below that figure, and per report, is loved and appreciated by its members.

I think the smartest route for those not planning to invest for the price of God Mode would be to get the Secret Pattern Masterclass (wait for a sale price of course) and sign up for the Elite Trading Club. They should also do the Bulletproof Strategy. This would be the best way to get perfect at 20-Minute Trading the fastest, and affordably.

The ongoing support provided by the Elite Trading Club is next-level and brings about the highest likelihood of success. I recommend watching the Bulletproof Strategy, which is 10 to 15 minutes of videos, once per month, so as not to fall prey to losing a ton of dough on silly but universally common mistakes.

Whatever path you take, please know there are only two reasons I went into teaching people this method. First is the pure and simple intention to help others do well and give non-professionals a chance to have an edge on the market using a realistic and simple strategy designed for busy people. The second reason was to create a business out of it so that all of the hard work my fellow frontierspeople and I did to make this system work for ourselves could add an additional source of income through course and service sales while making the services as affordable as possible so that the relationship between customer and provider is mutually beneficial.

Chapter 23
Everyone Needs a Frank

J ust as I needed Frank there to help me at the beginning of my journey, answer my questions, and walk me through things with simple explanations, so does everyone else. Since publishing my methodology, I have made available as much as possible live and instant help to those wanting to learn it. I have been paying customer service reps for the last year and a half to be there, well-trained, helpful, and informative for all questions and assistance required for anyone, even free course students, to be able to learn and practice 20-minute trading.

I, of course, cannot predict or envision precisely what the scene will be like years from now. However, if the courses I make and teach are still on the market, I will ensure that there will always be helpful and well-trained folks there to assist, just like Frank did for me and continues to do to this day, whenever I need it.

Feel free to take advantage of the customer service team's availability. They are there for you.

Chapter 24
Confession

I don't love the field of trading and have never wanted this to be my profession. But I had just spent two decades living on low wages, trying to see if I could help people in their lives, and I know I did because they tell me I did, and I believe them.

Any field can have unethical people and ethical people. For example, lawyers can be totally bereft of morals and ethics and spend all their time trying to get guilty criminals free of accountability or jail time. Some lawyers can change the lives of millions of people by confronting severely suppressive issues that plague our society, such as drug or chemical companies that have hidden results of harm caused so they could make billions. There is a spectrum in every field of good to bad. Some fields lend themselves to more bad folks than other fields do. Trading is one of them.

We get the image of the Wolf of Wall Street and his antics, taking advantage of regular, everyday folks who buy into penny stocks with a near guarantee that it will rocket up and make them tons of money; meanwhile, in reality, they lost in almost all instances, while the broker, the Wolf and his team, raked in commissions like they had a shop vac.

Even doctors can be unethical, even though most people who become doctors do so out of an innate desire to help people. There is yet a spectrum there as well of good to bad.

Trading can also bring about non-productive laziness, in which the successful trader does little to help the world turn better. But they simply make extra money, spend it on stupid crap, and help no one.

I hope to bring about a tasteful and ethical way to trade that favors the productive person who wants to fortify their family and augment their life with an additional source of income while carrying on being a vital part of society.

There are millions upon millions of people not working in the United States. Retired, welfare, imprisoned, and many other categories, and many of them cannot work. Society is carried on the backs of producers. I want to empower those people. I am not saying that retired or disabled people should be ignored, not in the least! That is not my point. But they would have the time to find even better methods than this one, which could take hours per day, and they could become more professional in it than those who must work. My point is that my focus is on the producer, the hard worker, and that category of folks who specifically inspired me to release and create this. They deserve a break and deserve to be supported as much as possible. From what I could tell, the only way to benefit from trading up until this was to make it a several-hour per-day activity, which means most hard-working people, especially those with a family, would not be able to do it.

When I stumbled across the field of trading, I felt like it was icky. But then I found a way to make it fun, responsible, and helpful. It's kind of like the graphics processing units made by AMD and Nvidia that were propelled by video games, and are now used in AI, medicine, architecture, movies, self-driving cars, and other incredible applications. I'm not a huge supporter of video game playing in excess. However, the companies that facilitated the augmentation of video game playing were able to fund the acceleration of other worthy exploits. And to clarify, I am not an anti-gamer or an activist against video games at all. Many of my best friends are gamers, and I even love watching them sometimes, like a sport. It's just not something I would consider healthy to do in excess.

I feel like I found a way to make trading accessible to productive people, and I feel I have accomplished a certain portion of my mission in this venture.

But going back to the first thing I brought up at the beginning of this chapter, I worked hard for 22 years dedicated to helping others while bringing in meager wages. And when it was time for me to have a fuller life and a family, I was not going to have internal arguments with my conscience about the method of arrival to a financial state I feel I certainly would have obtained through career means over a decade or two, aside from it being honest and legal.

But I am an artist. I wrote a fiction novel called *Four Leaf*, have drawn a number of pictures that I am proud of, made creative efforts in film and video, and more than anything, I love helping others in any way I can. I am thankful for the degree that this business and this trading technique allow me to do these things. Like I said, this is not my plan for a lifetime career. It is a fast energy source that should allow me to carry out other dreams and endeavors.

I hope these lessons allow me to lay my coat on the puddle for you to safely walk onto the road of your own goals and dreams.

Glossary

ASK (noun):   The price at which a position is offered for sale.

BID (noun):   An amount for which a buyer proposes to purchase a security, like in an auction.

BROKERAGE (noun):   A bank, an entity, or a company that holds one's money and places purchases and sales on one's behalf (Like E*TRADE, Robinhood, TD Ameritrade, IBKR, etc.). A brokerage account is like a bank account in which a client's money is held with the brokerage for use in purchases and sales at the client's order.

BUY (verb):   To purchase a security; n. the purchase of a security.

BUY ORDER (noun):   An order placed through one's brokerage for a security, whether or not the order has been filled.

BUY POINT (noun):   The exact moment that the position is purchased.

BUY SIGNAL (noun):   The indication that it is time to buy, as the share price is likely about to give a rally of some undetermined degree.

CALL OPTION (noun):   A risky financial instrument in which an options trader metaphorically "rents" another's 100 shares for a specified period and gets a profit or loss attendant upon the share price change over that period, similar to actually owning the shares. In actuality, it is a contract that a trader can buy to reserve the exclusive right to purchase 100 shares of a shareholder's stock for a specified coupon price for a specified period. The shareholder is obligated to sell their shares at this price if or when the contract holder demands it. They may not sell these 100 shares to anyone else but must "set them aside" for the exclusive privilege of the contract holder to buy if so desired.

This contract may then be resold, ideally for a higher price than purchased. It can also be used to buy the 100 shares in full for a lower price than the going market rate, thus gaining a profit.

CLOSE/CLOSED: **1.** (noun) the point when the US market is done for the day (EST 4 p.m., PST 1 p.m.); **2.** (verb) to sell a position or security that one owns. Some platforms refer to this as "sell to close" and its opposite is "buy to open."

CONTRACT PRICE (noun):   The amount for which an options trader paid or sold the option contract.

COST BASIS (noun):   What you paid originally for a particular security. This appears in one's portfolio when viewing a position. When it comes to option contracts, your cost basis is the contract price divided by 100.

Example: If you bought an option contract for $805.00, your cost basis would be 8.05. And you would use this cost basis to set your limit sell order (8.20) and your stop loss order (7.70) for example. (See also **CONTRACT PRICE.**)

DOW (noun):   The Dow Jones Industrial Average (DJIA), also known as the Dow 30, is a stock market index that tracks 30 large, publicly owned blue-chip companies trading on the New York Stock Exchange (NYSE) and NASDAQ. The Dow Jones is named after Charles Dow, who created the index in 1896, along with his business partner, Edward Jones.

EXECUTED (verb): The Buy Order or Sell Order has been carried out. This means the same as Filled and will usually appear on a notification or banner from the brokerage alerting one that an order has been carried out.

EXPIRY DATE (noun): The date that the option, or right, to transact shares at the strike price expires, at which point the investor that bought the contract can no longer exercise the right to buy the shares.

FILLED (verb): The transaction has gone through on a Buy Order or a Sell Order.

HERO RALLY (noun): A rally that looks like the flight of Superman into the sky. A big rally.

INDEX (noun): An index is a method to track the performance of a group of assets in a standardized way. Indexes typically measure the performance of a basket of securities intended to replicate a certain area of the market.

INSTRUMENT (noun): Trading instruments are assets or contracts that can be traded. Also see **SECURITIES**. Examples of trading instruments include options, commodity futures, stocks, CFDs, currencies, etc.

LIMIT ORDER (noun): When placing a Buy Order or a Sell Order, the investor is asked to choose an "Order Type." A Limit Order allows the investor to place a floor price for a security's sale or a ceiling for a security's purchase. If Limit is chosen, the investor is asked for the Limit Price. The brokerage will carry out the order without going lower than this Limit Price for the sale of a position or higher than this for the purchase of a security.

MARK (noun): Means the same as Mid, but is used in view of one's positions when estimating the current profit or loss of a security. Example: If one purchased ABC stock for $115, and the current going Mid (the center value between the bid and ask) is $118, then when viewing one's position on this security the word Mark will be used to communicate to you, the investor, the going rate for your security, in this case, $118. There will also be a column or category that says "Profit/Loss or P/L," which, in our example of having purchased a stock at $115 and now its current Mark is $118, would be "plus $3."

USAGE: (difference between Mid and Mark) Mid and Mark mean the same thing. The difference is where one uses these terms. Mid is used to estimate the value of a security when placing a Buy or Sell Order. Mark is used when viewing a position and determining its profit or loss.

MARKET ORDER (noun):   Is an "Order Type" an investor may select, in which the brokerage will make the transaction at the highest bid available for the sale of a position or at the lowest ask available for the purchase of a security. In essence, one placing a market order is willing to make the transaction at the going market rate rather than attempting to get a more profitable value for the trade.

USAGE: Limit and Market are the two main order types one will interact with. One will select Limit Orders to regulate how much one spends on something or how much one sells something for, so as to prevent losing money unnecessarily. One selects Market if one needs to get out of a position fast by selling it and is willing to lose some money to do so.

MID (noun):   The middle point between the highest bid and lowest ask, simply the mathematical middle between these two numbers. Example: If a shareholder asks $101 per share and a buyer bids $99 per share, the Mid is $100.

USAGE: Mid is used when one is placing an order to buy or sell. An investor intends to buy ten shares of ABC stock. The investor looks at the order page, where the highest bid and the lowest ask are listed, as well as the Mid between these two values. This Mid number is the agreed upon estimated amount the investor will spend.

USAGE: (difference between Mid and Mark) Mid and Mark mean the same thing. The difference is where one uses these terms. Mid is used to estimate the value of a security when placing a Buy or Sell Order. Mark is used when viewing a position and determining its profit or loss.

OCO (One-Cancels-Other) (noun): A sell order type with two orders placed on the same position at the same time. One to sell at a Limit if its value rises to a specific number, and the other to sell at a Stop Loss if it drops to a specified number. If the position's value hits either of these, the order will fill and cancel the other simultaneously. One Cancels the Other = OCO.

Example: I buy a share of Apple for $150. I place an OCO, with a Limit of $155 and a Stop Loss of $145, using OCO. The share price rises to $155, the brokerage auto-sells the share for $155 and cancels the stop loss at the same time. Had it dropped in value to $145, the brokerage would have sold the position for around 145 and canceled the Limit Order.

OPEN ORDER (noun): A Buy Order or a Sell Order which has not been filled. NOTE: When looking at one's list of orders on the trading platform, if a Buy Order or Sell Order has not been filled, the word "Open" will be displayed on this order in the portfolio.

PORTFOLIO (noun): A list of one's positions, their original cost, their current value, and how they are performing in terms of profit or loss.

POSITIONS (noun): Each security one owns is a Position. A list of one's securities and their current status and value are one's *positions*. Under each position is information such as the original amount spent, the current value, and the profit or loss.

RALLY (noun): Rapid increase in stock prices. A rally occurs when investors begin buying one or more stocks in large amounts, which represents an increase in demand and therefore raises the price.

RETAIL INVESTOR (noun): An individual investor who buys and sells securities for their own account. Some brokerage firms specialize in serving retail investors while other brokerage firms strive to attract business from institutions that engage in large trades.

SECURITIES (noun):   A tradeable investment; proofs of owner-ship, certificates of ownership, or titles of ownership that have a value and can be bought or sold as commodities. Stocks, options, and bonds are securities. The original meaning of "security," which dates back to the mid-15th century, was property pledged to guaran-tee some debt or promise of the owner. Starting in the 17th century, the word came to be used for a document evidencing a debt and eventually for any document representing a financial investment. By the late 19th century, the word could refer to any tradeable investment.

SELL (verb):   To place the sale of a security one owns for a price and the ensuing transfer of ownership upon payment; (noun) the act of selling a security.

SELL OFF (noun):   The rapid sale of a security by a large num-ber of holders. This increases the supply of the security available for sale and therefore drives down the price. Sell-offs occur for a num-ber of reasons. A stock may drop suddenly in price if its company issues a negative earnings report, if there are reports of a new tech-nology rendering the company's product obsolete, or if the compa-ny's costs rise. Sell-offs also happen for other, perhaps less rational reasons. For example, a natural disaster, which does not affect sup-plies, can still cause a sell-off.

SELL ORDER (noun):   An order placed through one's brokerage to sell a position, whether or not the order has been filled.

SPREAD (noun):   The monetary difference between the Bid and the Ask on a position, whether stocks or options. The spread is sim-ply how much money, dollars or cents, separate the *Bid* and *Ask* of any security.

STOP LOSS (noun):   An order with the brokerage to sell your position if it ever drops to an exactly stated value of your choosing.

Example: Your position's share price is currently worth $150. You place a stop loss for $145, and if the price drops that low, the brokerage sells it off, usually at a price just below the value of the stop loss you placed. With options, you can do the same. If the cost basis is 1.65 you could place a stop loss at 1.55. The brokerage will sell it off as close to 1.55 as it can, usually 1 to 4 cents below.

On E*TRADE, this type of order is listed as a *Stop on Quote*.

STRIKE PRICE (noun):   The reservation price for the 100 shares in an option contract.

TERM (noun):   How long an order will remain Open before self-canceling.

TRAILING STOP (TS) (noun):   An automatically adjusting stop loss sell order that rises along with the rising value of a position. When placing a trailing stop order, one is asked for the *Trailing Amount*. The trader selects how much they want the trailing amount to be, and the brokerage automatically adjusts the stop loss to be that exact amount below the value of the position in real time. If the position rises, the stop loss does as well. If the position falls, the stop loss *does not*.

Example. If one bought a stock at $150 and placed a trailing stop of $5, the brokerage would automatically set a stop loss for $145. But if the share price jumped to $155, the brokerage automatically sets a stop loss for $150, $5 less than $155. If the stock price drops to $151, the stop loss would remain at $150. It never goes down, only up. If the share price jumps to $157, a new stop loss would automatically be set for $152. In E*TRADE, this type of sell order is listed as *Trailing Stop $*.

This feature allows the trader to capitalize on a rally, which goes up-up-up, drops a little, goes up-up-up, and so on, only stopping at the position if it drops far enough. It has the liability, though, of often selling much further below the stated stop loss value, sometimes eliminating earned profit. This drop is called *slippage*.

YTD (YEAR-TO-DATE) (noun):   The overall profit or loss on the account shown that you have from January 1 of this year to the present.

About the Author

Jeremy Russell's life is a combination of ambition, creativity, and a commitment to sharing knowledge. Anchored in the city of Los Angeles, Jeremy runs his businesses and spends time with his friends and family.

From bustling LA, Jeremy's upbringing was enriched by his close-knit family. Growing up alongside his brothers, Brent and Kris, and his sister, Alexandra, Jeremy was nurtured by the values instilled by his parents, Michael and Helen. These familial bonds remain at the core of his journey.

Jeremy's early passions spanned the realms of entertainment, sports, and art. As a child actor, he stepped onto the stage of creativity, fostering a love for storytelling that endures to this day. An athlete and an artist during his school years, he developed a multidimensional perspective that would shape his future endeavors.

While pursuing architecture studies at UC Berkeley, Jeremy's creative impulse found expression in the world of design. This foundation laid the groundwork for his later ventures, where he would bridge creativity and practicality in innovative ways.

Embarking on a journey of service, Jeremy devoted over two decades to work through non-profit organizations. This period of altruism reinforced his belief in the power of collective action and kindled a desire to make a lasting difference in the lives of others.

Amid his diverse pursuits, Jeremy's literary talents came to fruition in the form of *Four Leaf*, a captivating military thriller. His ability to craft compelling narratives immerses readers in worlds both familiar and entertaining.

Jeremy's artistic range extends beyond the written word, manifesting in his intricate pencil drawings, reflecting his meticulous attention to detail. These visual creations are showcased on his website, artbyjeremy.com, where his passion for fine arts finds expression.

Guided by a vision of empowerment, Jeremy is the driving force behind 20-Minute Trader®, where he leads with a mission to equip aspiring traders with practical strategies. The 20-Minute Trader methods empower individuals to navigate the complexities of the stock market, harnessing success while maintaining life's balance. To connect with Jeremy's expertise, reach out at info@20mintrader.com or follow him on Instagram @20mintrader.

Additionally, Jeremy heads jBot LLC, channeling his innovation into creating trading algorithms and bots. This venture underscores his commitment to leveraging technology for efficient trading practices.

Jeremy Russell's journey is one that resonates with the ambitious, the creative, and the compassionate. Through family, artistry, community engagement, and innovative entrepreneurship, he embodies the spirit of impacting both the trading world and the lives of those he is lucky to contact.

Index